Praise for *The Practicing*

"Where does great performance really come from. Thomas Sterner knows — and he sees how profound the answer is."
— **Geoff Colvin**, author of *Talent Is Overrated*

"I use the techniques I have learned from *The Practicing Mind* every day. The approach is relevant for both business executives and their junior golf children on and off the course. I recommend it to all my students because its lessons will help them in both golf and life."
— **Eric MacCluen**, PGA Professional and Director of Golf Instruction at Applecross Country Club

"Thomas Sterner gives us a useful, thoughtful, much-needed book on the often-overlooked science and art of practice. It blends careful research with plenty of enlightening and entertaining personal stories. Anyone hoping to excel at anything should read this. Keep on practicing!"
— **Roy F. Baumeister**, coauthor of *Willpower: Rediscovering the Greatest Human Strength*

"As you embrace the process-oriented approach described in *The Practicing Mind*, you'll achieve better results in any endeavor."
— **Michael J. Gelb**, author of *How to Think Like Leonardo da Vinci* and *Brain Power*

"Thomas Sterner...shares insights, stories, and advice for mastering the skills of our choosing with less frustration and more pleasure."
— *New Thought*

"Sterner's encouragement...is to find things that help us do well and practice them — staying in the moment, creating and practicing good habits, and being patient, disciplined, and even-tempered in our work."

— *The Horn Call*

"Thomas Sterner's brilliance shines through in the brevity of this complex book's pages....This tiny but intense book delivers enough information to contemplate and apply for a lifetime."

— *Roundtable Reviews*

Praise for Thomas M. Sterner's Work

"I do not say this lightly and it's no exaggeration. Thomas Sterner's work on practice has changed my life. As a Master Life Coach Instructor I have read many materials on self-help, mind management, habit development, and growth. I rate Tom's work to be among the very best of the hundreds of books I have studied. He teaches his brilliant concepts in a style that is easy to understand and implement. It doesn't matter what you want to get better at doing or being; Tom has the teachings that, when applied, will get you there. I give Tom my highest recommendation. Study his work, learn and practice what he demonstrates, and you'll know more peace, productivity, and profit, guaranteed."

— **Brooke Castillo**, Master Certified Coach and president of The Life Coach School

IT'S JUST A THOUGHT

Also by Thomas M. Sterner

The Practicing Mind

Fully Engaged

IT'S JUST A THOUGHT

Emotional Freedom through Deliberate Thinking

THOMAS M. STERNER

New World Library
Novato, California

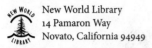
New World Library
14 Pamaron Way
Novato, California 94949

Text design by Tona Pearce Myers

Library of Congress Cataloging-in-Publication Data

Names: Sterner, Thomas M., date, author.
Title: It's just a thought : emotional freedom through deliberate thinking / Thomas M. Sterner.
Description: Novato, California : New World Library, [2023] | Includes biblio-graphical references. | Summary: "The author explores the ultimate motives of human behavior and the ways we can consciously shape our own thoughts and habits through greater self-awareness. Readers will learn the mechanics involved to master their thinking and become the thinkers of their thoughts instead of the ones 'being thought.'"-- Provided by publisher.
Identifiers: LCCN 2022050248 (print) | LCCN 2022050249 (ebook) | ISBN 9781608688296 (paperback) | ISBN 9781608688302 (epub)
Subjects: LCSH: Thought and thinking. | Awareness. | Self-actualization (Psychology)
Classification: LCC BF441 .S7754 2023 (print) | LCC BF441 (ebook) | DC 153.4/2--dc23/eng/20221116
LC record available at https://lccn.loc.gov/2022050248
LC ebook record available at https://lccn.loc.gov/2022050249

First printing, February 2023
ISBN 978-1-60868-829-6
Ebook ISBN 978-1-60868-830-2
Printed in Canada on 100% postconsumer-waste recycled paper

New World Library is proud to be a Gold Certified Environmentally Responsible Publisher. Publisher certification awarded by Green Press Initiative.

10   9   8   7   6   5   4   3   2   1

This book is dedicated to my daughters, Margie and Melissa. How fortunate is a man to be blessed by two such wonderful souls choosing him as their father in their journey through this life. You are both my best friends.

Contents

Introduction

If I were to ask you the simple question, "Are you happy?" what would your answer be? How would you know? Where does the information come from that lets you answer my question accurately and honestly? Your answer might be, "Well, sometimes I am and sometimes I'm not. Sometimes I'm sad and sometimes I'm angry."

Does the information that tells you how you feel always come from the same place? Do you know where that place is, and do you have any control over it, or does it just happen to you regardless of what you would prefer to experience? What *is* happiness, sadness, or anger? I think we can define them as feelings or emotions that are preceded by and intertwined with our thoughts.

When you "think," you create a thought, but where does emotion come from? Is it an inseparable part of the thought? For example, when you feel anxious, you are having anxious thoughts. So is the anxiety "in" the thought, or do you have a choice of how you interpret and experience the content of the thought? The answer is yes. You do. If the experience of the thought were absolute, then everyone who had that thought would feel the same way, but we know that isn't true. If I told you that tomorrow you must stand up and speak in front of a thousand people, depending on who you are, your response may be to experience horrific anxiety, but the same thought might make someone else very excited. The thought and the situation are the same, but each person's interpretation of the thought is very different, and so are the emotions that are experienced.

When I was growing up in the 1960s and 1970s, I often heard adults comment, "Well, you just can't control your emotions or your feelings." I was captive in a world where people actually believed that. In those days, there really was no such thing as neuroscience to prove otherwise, and disciplines such as psychology were quite primitive. Today, we have come to understand much more regarding how our minds work and why we think and act as we do, but what we now claim as cutting-edge information is actually not new. So much of what we are now discovering has been common knowledge in Eastern thought systems for centuries, but when I was growing up, our Western empirical scientific methods had not yet produced the hard research data that would allow us in the West to invest our belief in the internal experiences that those in the East were describing.

So again, is it possible for us to choose not only how we interpret our thoughts but even what thoughts we have? The answer is yes. We live in a wonderful time where our understanding of the different aspects of our mind — the conscious, the unconscious, and the subconscious — gives us the tools necessary to become a super thinker, someone who can say, "I use my thoughts and I don't allow my thoughts to use me." This gift, this skill, has always been possible, but for those in the West, it has only presented itself through our ever-expanding research in very recent decades. This book explores what we now know about why we behave as we do and how to develop the skill to craft the behavioral changes we desire. We will learn the mechanics involved to master our thinking and become the thinker of our thoughts instead of the one "being thought."

For me, it has been a decades-long journey to discover and understand that most of the time we are victims of our "automated thinking" rather than the master creators of our thoughts. To truly appreciate the power that our current science offers, I feel we need to look back in time just a little bit to better understand how far we have come, and I will share some of how my journey into this fascinating study has evolved.

Many in my parents' generation grew up very poor during the Great Depression. At that time, finishing high school was generally considered a full education. Knowledge of the East and how their philosophies viewed the world was totally outside of their experience. It should come as no surprise then that, when I was growing up, it was outside of my experience as well. Then, during my freshman year in college, a close friend gave me the text-book from his "Philosophies of the World" course and told me, "I think you'll enjoy this." Well, he was right. I couldn't put the book down. For hundreds of pages, it described the history and concepts of the different Eastern and Western thought systems. This was the beginning of my understanding of why I was so impatient to reach my goals and why so many times I gave up on them. It was the catalyst that changed my whole concept of how I could experience accomplishing any goal, even a task that I wasn't particularly fond of. It started me along the path of rewriting my internal programming, which changed me from being an extremely undisciplined young adult with a constantly agitated and scattered mind into someone who was referred to as always calm and one of the most disciplined and focused people my friends and family had ever known. The difference it made in how I experienced life was extraordinary, and this catalyst sparked the need to write my first book, *The Practicing Mind*.

As a working adult, after I finished college in the late 1970s, I began noticing that the Western business model, with its attachment to profits, was collapsing in its ability to compete in the global marketplace and even on our own soil in America. That model was obsessed with the *moment* that the goal was reached as opposed to the *process* of achieving it. The process was seen as a necessary inconvenience that had to be endured at best, and certainly not as the hidden key to success.

American automobile makers, once kings of the industry, were struggling to match the consistent dependability that Japanese car makers produced. The average consumer took notice and was willing to pay for that quality and consistency. At that time, my industry was the piano business, and Japanese pianos were of such superior quality that they put all but a few American piano manufacturers out of business. At the turn of the twentieth century, there were over three hundred piano manufacturers in the United States. By the 1980s, there were just a few. American piano retailers were fighting to get Japanese brands on their floor to sell because without them they couldn't compete. All the piano retailers had to do was open up a Japanese piano and show the customer the quality of the workmanship, as compared to an American piano, and the sale was done. A piano is a lifetime investment, and the relatively small additional price for a Japanese brand was irrelevant. American piano manufacturers were either clueless or unwilling to deal with the reasons why their products were inferior.

Japanese pianos only came in a few cabinet styles, black and a few generic wood finishes. This was because the Japanese viewed the piano first and foremost as a musical instrument. After all, when you purchased a violin, you didn't ask if they had it in cherry or walnut. You just wanted a superior instrument. American manufacturers, in contrast, tried to bolster their falling sales by offering their instruments in many cabinet styles, like a piece of furniture, and treating the fact that it was a musical instrument almost as an afterthought. They missed the point, and the difference in quality became so great that piano technicians sometimes joked that American pianos were made out of the crates that Japanese pianos were shipped in. Since then, the American piano industry has never recovered. Through the 1980s the electronics industry followed a similar path. During this same period, all the popular, high-end stereo systems, the ones considered status symbols, were made in Japan.

How were the Japanese able to create such a total and legitimate monopoly in the marketplace? The magic formula was really quite simple. The Japanese operated under a completely different mindset. They focused on the process of creating the instrument, the car, or the stereo components instead of the perceived end product. Conversely, the American mantra was, "We can't be paid until it's made, so get it done." In other words, the process of manufacturing the product was viewed as a necessary exercise, one that cost money and should be expedited and trimmed down to its bare essentials so that the profit from sales could be realized as quickly as possible. The goal was to make as many as possible in the least amount of time and at the lowest cost.

In contrast, in Japan, you worked a manufacturing job for life, and the expectation was for perfect work, not the quantity produced, and you were given the time to accomplish that. As I mention in *The Practicing Mind*, a retailer friend of mine who toured one of the Japanese piano plants was stunned when he asked a worker how many of his particular components he had to complete in a day. The worker, somewhat confused by the question, replied, "As many as I can make perfect." Coming from a Western mindset, the retailer asked, "Doesn't your supervisor pressure you if you don't produce a certain quota?"

"What is a supervisor?" the worker asked.

"Someone who makes sure you do your job," the retailer replied.

The worker said, "Why would I need someone to do that? This is my job."

I think it is obvious, especially when compared to the work environment we experience today, that this worker represented a completely different paradigm, one that worked very well. Japanese products were exquisite, and the workers loved their jobs.

During those days, in the Olympics, sports such as archery were sometimes dominated by Asian countries, in part because of this fundamentally different mindset, which focuses on the *process* of drawing the bow rather than on *hitting* a bull's-eye. In this mindset, the target simply gets in the way of the arrow. This mindset helps us operate at our highest potential.

Beginning in the early 1980s, the Western mindset began to shift. The Western mind was more comfortable trusting its *science* rather than thought systems from other cultures. In reality, those thought systems *were* the science of Eastern cultures, and they were proven through thousands of years of focusing on the internal world of the individual and by observing, or perhaps I should say gathering data about, how that aspect of the human condition worked. I have always felt that both perspectives are two sides of the same coin. Modern Western science is not very old, dating back only several hundred years, and it has taken some time for it to catch up and come to the same conclusions as Eastern thought systems. This is good for those of us in the West because we are much more comfortable believing in concepts that we tell ourselves are based on "facts." In the end, though, both perspectives, both truths, are driven by observations that can be validated. In the East, those validations occur more through personal conscious experiences that can't necessarily be shared directly with nonparticipants. In the West, validation comes from experiments that prove theories and hypotheses to be true.

For example, I recently read a study on the different brain wave states. The purpose of the study was to better understand what effect, if any, the practice of meditation has on our brains. Are those effects positive or negative, and are the effects consistent in the level of impact they produce from one practitioner to another?

You may be familiar with nomenclature such as theta, alpha, and beta brain waves. They represent different brain wave frequencies that coincide with our waking and sleeping states. A group of scientists wanted to study what they called Olympic meditators. Most of the practitioners were monks from Tibet because they meditate for long hours every day as part of their daily discipline, but others were everyday people like you and me. The requirement was that they had to be very experienced in practicing meditation because the study was looking to quantify the real potential benefits of meditation. The study's main author commented that most people only reach the gamma state of brain waves for one or two seconds at a time during the day. They were stunned to find that the practitioners they were studying basically *lived* in the gamma state. One of the scientists involved in the study said, "We can't even begin to imagine what that must be like."

My point is that for centuries these practitioners have been quietly experiencing this level of brain function, and what they have been experiencing is unarguably real. But there was no way for them to prove that to an outside observer. Any attempt to do that would have been futile anyway. After all, real conscious "knowing" begins and ends in direct experience. Can you describe what it feels like to be in love to someone who has never experienced that blessing? Can you describe the sound of the ocean surf to someone who has never seen the ocean? Ironically, it could be argued that Western fact-based science is just as obscure. So much of the science that we accept as fact is constantly changing, and many times the proof that is so obvious to a physicist is in the form of a mathematical equation that very few others can understand.

In 1985, an eight-week series appeared on public television called *The Day the Universe Changed*. It was hosted by science historian James Burke. I watched the whole series, and it was fascinating. The series recounted specific transformational events in history, such as when the Gutenberg printing press was invented and how making books available to the masses impacted the world, since it both forced and gave a reason for more people to become literate.

At the end of the last episode, the host was standing outside a monastery in the mountains of Tibet. You could hear the monks singing the primordial sound of "Om" inside. It has been said that Om is the sound of the universe idling, and in deep states of meditation you can actually hear it. Whether you agree with that or not, don't forget that just because you have not experienced something doesn't mean it is not true or doesn't exist. With the monk's chanting in the background, host James Burke said: "Their view of the world and how it works has been the same for thousands of years. Our view of the world and how it works changes almost every day, and every day it gets closer and closer to theirs." So many years later that statement has become even more true as our understanding of quantum mechanics deepens.

We have come so far in the last thirty years in our understanding of how our mind works, how the universe works, our relationship to it, and the impact that our thoughts, which feel so private, have not only on us, our body, and our health but also on those around us and the world at large. Scientific instruments can now map out different areas of our brain and show which areas light up in relation to what we are thinking and feeling. Instruments can watch our heart talk to our brain. Yes, the heart stores memories and has its own type of nervous system. It remembers feelings. We have all kinds of numbers, charts, and data that allow us to believe in invisible phenomena even though we may have never experienced something ourselves. Through our science, we now feel more comfortable talking about, even investigating, these areas of human potential without feeling like others will see us as peculiar. Meditation has become quite commonplace, and it's being taught in schools and businesses all over the world. Its benefits are widely documented and accepted. I once read an article where the head of a transnational corporation said something to the effect of: "If you're not meditating every day, you're making bad decisions."

But having this awareness and harnessing it as an individual to expand your potential in unimaginable ways are two different things. We must change old habits and introduce new, better ones. With all this new knowledge of how we interface with each other and the universe come an opportunity *and* a responsibility not only to advance ourselves to another level of consciousness but to raise the consciousness of everyone around us, as well as to recognize that we are much more alike than we are different.

Change is necessary, since the way we have been carrying on is clearly not working. If this beautiful earth is to continue to be our home and the home for those yet to come, we need to put forth an effort. That effort requires discipline. Effort is just exerted energy. We experience this as struggle only when we infuse effort with the wrong emotions.

I have learned that mental discipline is power and freedom. It's the real currency in our lives because without it we are not in control of what we are feeling. But what is discipline? Is it just the ability to do something that we don't feel like doing? In my experience, the answer is no. Discipline is the skill of being able to shift our attention into the present moment. When we don't feel like doing something, it's because we *feel* like doing something else, and that something else is not where we are in the moment. When we have the ability to release ourselves from being attached to doing something we can only do at a different time and to immerse ourselves in the present moment, in the process of what we are doing right here and right now, we free ourselves from feelings of anxiety, impatience, and frustration. These feelings are inherent in the experience of anticipating a future moment, something desired but yet to be acquired. What we call discipline begins to flow naturally, and we stop fighting and resisting this moment.

Sometimes I am asked, "If you are practicing being fully present, being process- and not product-oriented, is that mindfulness?" My reply is that mindfulness is a component of what I call the "practicing mind," but the practicing mind is much more. It would be more accurate to say the practicing mind is the skill that enables you to enjoy the *process of becoming* mindful; once mastered, that skill can be aimed at anything. Mindfulness is also a skill, and as with all skills, you need to learn the mechanics, and they must be repeated until they become natural and free-flowing. This is important to understand because it drastically impacts your experience of transformation and expansion. When you possess the practicing mind, you stop pushing against yourself as you work at change. Instead, you surrender to the moment, and you feel content with who you are and where you are in this moment. You feel that you are where you should be and doing what you should be doing right now.

The purpose of this book is to give you an overview of the relationship between you, your mind, and what you experience as your thoughts. I hope to increase your awareness of who you really are so that you can step on your own path of enlightenment and find peace, joy, calmness, and power. Our world needs for you to understand your energy and to be more in control of it. This is a very pivotal time. Clearly, it is one of the most stressful in history, but it also offers opportunities that before were much more elusive.

For thousands of years, people wanted to fly. They were good people — educated, determined, courageous, and hardworking. Yet every attempt failed and quite a few people perished in their effort. The reason for this was not because humans were not meant to fly or because we were incapable of flight. The reason was because we did not understand what we now call Bernoulli's principle. Put simply, this principle describes how the shape of a wing creates lift as it moves through the air. Before discovering this principle, people erroneously thought by watching birds that it was the flapping of the wings that allowed them to fly. That motion actually creates thrust, not lift. Films of the early failures show people with boards strapped to their arms jumping off of various precipices and plummeting downward regardless of how hard they flapped their arms.

Seen from the side, a bird's wing has a curved top. Because of this, as the wing moves through the air, the air is split. Some of the air goes over the top of the wing and some goes underneath. The air that goes over the top of the wing has to travel farther than the air underneath because of the curvature. This creates lower pressure on the top of the wing, and hence lift is born.

Why is this relevant? Because once this was understood, flight took off (no pun intended) at an incredible rate. After thousands of years of failure, people needed only a few decades to develop airplanes that could fly at four hundred miles an hour at altitudes above twenty-five thousand feet, and not long after that we were going into space. Something similar has been happening over the past thirty years through our studies of quantum physics, the brain, and consciousness and how they all interact, which will have a transformational impact on us as a species. Things that seemed impossible before will become a natural part of life, even things we can't begin to imagine. We have the power to heal ourselves, to heal others, and to calm areas of conflict in the world by consciously creating and intentionally directing our thoughts. Even now this is being done on relatively small scales with proven results, but because of the lack of coverage in the mainstream media, it's not widely known. Our mainstream media doesn't focus on or share that sort of thing. But just like meditation, because of its immense value, it will become more and more accepted and commonplace, and we will move into a new era as we accept our true power and birthright. Take heart. Exciting and amazing times are ahead of us.

CHAPTER 1

Looking Back to Move Forward

Understanding the Path

A mantra I often ask clients to repeat is this: "I am not my thoughts. I have thoughts. Some thoughts I create but most I do not, and it is those thoughts that can unknowingly create me."

Leonardo da Vinci said, "There are those that know. There are those that know after they are shown. There are those that do not know."

When we understand and live in the perspective that we are not our thoughts, then we are the master of who we are and what we experience. However, when we do not know, and when we live within our thoughts, we are easily manipulated by the media, those around us, and even the programming that we ourselves have installed at one time or another in our subconscious. Getting to the place where we are both the observer and the master of our thinking is a skill like all things in life. However, this skill is rarely taught, at least in Western culture. But that doesn't mean we can't learn and master it.

When we are in this observer perspective, we can be conscious of it, and yet describing the experience is beyond the realm of linguistics. During a coaching session, a client once said to me, "I want to know what it feels like to go through the day as you. What does it feel like to experience the day as you do?" I said I would answer his question after he described the color blue to me. He looked at me with a contemplative face for just long enough to process the impossibility of my request and then smiled, saying, "Never mind, I get it."

The experience of referencing your life from the viewpoint of who you *really* are and not from the *programming* that has been installed, either knowingly or unknowingly by you or someone else, is beyond words. This conscious knowing is not unlike seeing a sunset or being in love. We know these perspectives only when we experience them personally. And like an artist, dancer, or musician, we increase our skill through practice, and the experience becomes deeper and easier to elicit on demand.

As da Vinci said, "There are those that know after they are shown." During a coaching session with a rather confident client, we were talking about the difference between the conscious mind and the subconscious mind. The client said he didn't agree with my assessment. He felt that *he* was always "thinking" his thoughts and that he was consciously creating them with *his* will. To make my point and give him a conscious experience of his own, I responded by telling him that I was the coach and he was the client. I said that he needed to sit there and keep his mouth shut until I told him to speak. As you would expect, his reaction was very predictable. His body language changed into a defensive posture. His facial expression was one of irritation and anger.

I asked him, "Did you consciously choose to create what you are experiencing right now? Do you like feeling the way you feel right now? Are you in control of how you feel right now?" I then explained that he had installed a response to my tone of voice in his subconscious long ago. It was sitting there on his hard drive, a file waiting to be executed. I merely gave him the stimulus that called it forth. I discuss this process in more detail in chapter 2.

I knew that this man, like most of us, lived most of his day being *in* his thoughts and not from a perspective of observing them, and his response to my words and tone reflected the emotional content of those thoughts. I knew he would relinquish his privilege of choice rather than respond as he would most like to. He probably wasn't even aware that he had a choice. He surrendered who he was and became a servant to a mind that was just playing a program that *it* thought was the response he wanted. Of course, I apologized for my comment and let him know that I certainly did not mean what I had said. I asked him to tell me how he was processing what we were talking about. His face softened, his shoulders relaxed, and he broke into a half smile, laughing to himself, and thanked me for such an incredible moment of awakening.

It has been seventeen years since my first book, *The Practicing Mind*, was published. I actually wrote that book about twenty-four years ago, but I didn't self-publish the first edition until 2005. I make that point because, since then, we have learned so much about how our mind works. We keep peeling away the mysterious layers of the nature of consciousness. Where does our mind end and we begin? Is there a difference?

I should also note that our minds were different back then. For the most part, they were not in such a state of constant turbulence, constant overstimulation. Cellphones were in a very infant state, and they weren't very "smart." You could make a phone call, that was it. Sometimes it worked and sometimes it didn't. If you made a call out of your service area, that was considered roaming and was charged extra. Today, of course, smartphones do much more than make phone calls. They connect us to any place, to any person, and to any source of information instantly, regardless of where in the world we happen to be. Combined with the internet, smartphones are a truly amazing technology. However, there is a downside that can be quite toxic. That technology works two ways. It gives the ever-expanding forms of media access to us twenty-four hours a day, seven days a week, because we are so connected, even addicted, to our phones.

I recently read an article by a sailor who made a telling

observation. He was vacationing in the Caribbean, sitting on his boat in a marina, when a few slips away, he noticed a family of four — a mother, father, and two young children below the age of twelve — sitting in the cockpit of their sailboat. An incredibly beautiful sunset was happening, the kind that only occurs in the islands, and yet it was going completely unnoticed by this family because each of them had their heads down, staring at their phones. No one was noticing. No one was talking. They were absorbed in their screens. What could have been more important on a screen than what was going on around them, what they had traveled who knows how far to experience?

The level of dysfunctionality that this scene evokes is difficult to comprehend, and sad to say, it is getting worse. For older people in my generation, we at least lived most of our lives without this technology, so it could be argued that we have a foundation that gives us some perspective, a point of comparison for how much things are changing. But for younger generations, it is all they know, and it is deteriorating their attention spans and their ability to imagine, for sure. The data doesn't lie.

Our brain is being given a constant stream of information to process and decode. This never-ceasing mental processing creates compulsive thinking. We can't turn it off. We struggle to just be still and fully engaged in an activity like reading a book for more than a few moments. The thoughts created by this nonstop thinking also unconsciously and involuntarily create our perspective of reality. Our constant connection to media gives others the power to affect and even dictate how we feel about ourselves, each other, and the world in general. But probably the worst part is that this loss of control *feels* normal.

Not too long ago I was teaching a class on present-moment functioning to a group of high school kids. I started off the session by telling them we were going to do a short task. I wanted them to close their eyes and stop thinking for just two minutes. I set a timer, said go, and all they had to do was close their eyes and stop thinking. When the time was up and I told them to open their eyes, they immediately began chattering. None of them had been able to stop thinking. Of course, this wasn't any surprise to me, but it was a moment of awakening for them.

Despite their lack of success, most of them still experienced a brief period of much-reduced thinking, and that was enough to make an impression. This was the first time in their lives that they had become the observers of what their minds were doing without their permission. I asked them what it meant if they were commanding their mind to stop thinking using their will and their mind was totally ignoring them. Since they looked somewhat confused, I rephrased the question and asked, "If you are telling your mind to stop thinking and it refuses to comply, who is really in control, because it's not you?"

I suggest you try this exercise for yourself right now: Stop reading, and set a timer for two minutes. Sit in a chair that has good back support. When you start the timer, close your eyes to reduce external distractions and take a few deliberate deep breaths. As you exhale, let your shoulders drop and feel your body relax. Now try to stop thinking and notice what happens. Very quickly your mind will get bored and go looking for something to think about. Just keep using your willpower to try and stop the process. You won't be able to stop the constant motion of your mind, but you will be able to slow it down, even if just a small amount.

This was truly a life-changing perspective for these young people, as was the experience of meditation itself. The hint of inner stillness where there was no anxiety, no anticipation of anything, and no judgment was very seductive and created in them a way of feeling they had never experienced before. Though they couldn't articulate it, it was a brief experience of "I am not my thoughts; some thoughts I do create, but most I do not." For a number of these young adults, this inspired them to develop a thought awareness practice that led to improvements in their personalities and their academic achievements, according to the parents who contacted me afterward.

The need to understand how our minds work and what the relationship is between *we* the observers and our minds is more important today than it has ever been. Division among people is growing as our minds become more agitated and filled with thoughts of fear and anger. These divisive thoughts are produced by unconscious, involuntary, and uncontrolled thinking. If we do not understand where our thoughts come from, and we are not in control of that process, then we become prisoners of ourselves, prisoners of our own thinking. Our thoughts dictate what we feel. Ask yourself: "If I didn't think, could I feel stress? Could I feel anxiety? Could I feel joy?" The answer is no because thought is the vehicle for all of these experiences. The thought happens, we interpret the thought, and then we experience the emotional content.

We need to change ourselves if we are going to change the world we live in and experience. Indeed, the path we are on is not sustainable if we wish to survive, if we wish to find joy in our lives, and if we wish to pass on the same opportunities we have been gifted to the next generations.

But change can be difficult. It requires getting off the path that we have ingrained and habitualized so deeply through thousands of repetitions of behaviors, thoughts, and interpretations. To do that we must understand the path we are on and how we created it. We need to know what our new path looks like and how to manifest it as effortlessly as possible. We must become attached to the process of achieving that change and to the concept of unlimited human expansion. This change is not a limited moment in the future when we will feel "now I am all that I need to be." Again, as with an artist, dancer, or musician, learning this skill requires knowledge of the mechanics and practice to develop proficiency. As our skill increases, our awareness of what we are truly capable of will become both deeper and easier to execute on demand. We will be the master of our mind instead of the victim of our involuntary and compulsive thinking. And our experience and understanding of that will reach others and help them on their own paths, which will spread to the others in their lives. We can define the experience of change as difficult, but as I have written in *The Practicing Mind* and *Fully Engaged*, words such as *difficult* and *struggle* are labels we attach to feelings. Those feelings are the result of our interpretations, which are neither absolute nor permanent. They are just reactions we have accepted as true and immutable.

Some people feel that this all sounds well and good in theory, but they insist that some things in life are inherently upsetting and there is absolutely nothing we can do about it. My response is, we shouldn't assume that because *we* don't have a particular skill, no one in the world can have it. Many people have skills that others don't, and like all skills, these can be learned through understanding the mechanics and proper practice. The experience of learning that skill can also be completely devoid of impatience and self-judgment. I have experienced this in every area of my life and through some of the most difficult and upsetting situations. I have also helped many others learn how to practice and execute this skill.

Recently, I was listening to an interview with a professional golfer who had just won a tour championship. I was so impressed and heartened by his perspective. I was, however, not surprised because his mindset is widely known in mental performance studies. He was asked what had changed in him that had given him the ability to accomplish such an incredible and difficult task. He commented that, in order to get results, we must first come up with a process we can fall in love with and then enjoy executing that process. He also commented on how much he enjoyed high-pressure situations because practicing the process had prepared him for them.

The practicing mind is a phrase I coined years ago when trying to come up with a way of describing the main component in functioning at our highest level. To reiterate, learning a skill, any skill — whether it be physical in nature, such as your golf swing, or emotional, such as how you handle a particular person or situation — in the shortest amount of time, with the least amount of effort, without a sense of struggle, and while being in love with the process *is* a skill in itself. Once learned, that skill is immensely self-empowering.

So exactly what is the practicing mind? Is it just another word for mindfulness? No, it is not. Mindfulness is in the practicing mind, but the practicing mind is not necessarily in mindfulness. What I mean is that being mindful is a skill, and the practicing mind is the skill of *learning to love the process of becoming mindful.* Accepting this truth, which has been documented in ancient philosophies and now proven through our empirical science, provides freedom from so many struggles. Understanding the mechanics of this and learning the joy that comes from this skill was my goal when I wrote *The Practicing Mind* and *Fully Engaged*. But once we have that skill, once we know what to practice and how to practice, what do we do with it? In other words, where do we *aim* that skill? What do we change in our life to maximize its usefulness? Without that awareness, we are like an archer who has learned the proper process of drawing the bow perfectly but still lacks the awareness of where to focus their energy.

It's Just a Thought is about the science of why we think certain thoughts that upset us. Why do we react to some situations in ways that cause us pain, anxiety, and fear? Why can't we just turn our mind off so we can have a break from the constant internal dialogue? Can we change any of this, and if so, how difficult is it to do? *It's Just a Thought* is about understanding how your conscious and subconscious minds interact with each other. Which one is really you, and which one is in charge? What is the relationship between your heart and your brain? Are you aware of the constant dialogue between them? What does that look like, and how does it affect how you feel? How much of your day are *you* really creating your thoughts? The answer might surprise you.

I titled this chapter "Looking Back to Move Forward: Understanding the Path" because discovering what we have learned about the workings of our minds gives us an understanding of where to aim our energy. If you are to be successful, if you are to enjoy being immersed in the process of executing those changes and having patience with your journey, you will require a practicing mind, a mind that is fully engaged.

Reading is a skill, and once that skill is mastered, you have a choice of where to direct that skill. Your mastery opens up a world of possibilities. You can read a romance novel for enjoyment. You can read a spiritual text for inspiration. You can even write a self-help book yourself. Such are the gifts of that skill. Having a practicing mind is very similar. It allows you to pursue any goal or approach any task with a perspective that in each moment is absorbed in the process of achievement and is fully experiencing that moment's purpose with joy and patience.

This book's purpose is to give you a better understanding of how you can use that skill to weather what we are all experiencing in the world today. It will help you to raise your own frequency and to pour that higher energy into the world's grid simply by just being yourself. Fear and anger are *not* who you are. They are just a thought, a response that you have learned to have when certain situations arise. You can learn a better way. Armed with the knowledge of where those thoughts come from and how to effect change, you become the master of your mind's capabilities instead of a servant to its rantings. You become much more of who you really are. So let's get started.

CHAPTER 2

Are You Thinking or Being Thought?

Who Is the Real You?

If you have done the two-minute "stop thinking" exercise in chapter 1, then you have directly experienced that you are not always in charge of what is going on in your head. That experience often begs the questions: "Who am I? Am I the one telling my mind to stop thinking or am I the one generating thoughts against my wishes?" That is what this chapter title is asking. The real you, the one who should be in charge, is the one with the will, the creative conscious thinker.

Unfortunately, most of us most of the time are in the programs being run by our subconscious minds. Instead of making conscious choices in the moment, we are nothing more than puppets of the thoughts and reactions our subconscious minds offer up instantly in every situation we encounter. Flipping the roles requires personal change, and trying to change aspects of our personality that aren't serving our happiness is more than just repeating new mechanics, such as executing new, predetermined reactions to old emotional triggers. In fact, I think the bigger challenge can be staying excited and motivated about change. That enthusiasm needs to be constantly refreshed and nurtured. Otherwise, the self-analyses that made us search for solutions and the inspiration that we felt we had found in those solutions can easily dissolve away, particularly during the initial period of the process. I know for myself that when I am in the process of changing a certain behavior, I must constantly be reminded of the mechanics that I need to practice. The ideas themselves are not so difficult to remember, but the old ways are so strong that they can overpower our recall of those ideas when we need them the most. The pushback of old habits is the strongest in the beginning of change.

The reason for this is that the person you are right now is the personality you have mastered. You have practiced your behavior over and over again, thousands of times, and at this point that behavior is fully installed into your subconscious mind. It is effortless even if it's exactly the way you *don't* want to be. I make this point because it's the reason that I repeat certain ideas and concepts over and over again as we go through this material. This way, they become ingrained into your consciousness and become a strong trigger that is pulled when you are confronted with the need to change your response. When the trigger is pulled, I want you to look at the situation as an *observer* first. I want you to see the situation as an *opportunity* to execute a new response that you have consciously decided, in moments of reflection and self-analysis, is a better way of handling that situation. I want you to get out ahead of your conditioned response so that you afford yourself the *privilege of choice* in the moment. Even if you feel you don't execute a new strategy perfectly or even well, being aware that you *have* a choice is the path to deliberate thinking. In itself, that is an important form of success. The rest is a matter of repetition and refining mechanics without judgment.

Viktor Frankl was a Viennese psychiatrist who spent most of World War II in a Nazi concentration camp, an experience he describes in his book *Man's Search for Meaning*. Frankl is often credited with the famous quote: "Between stimulus and response there is a space. In that space is our power to choose our response. In our response lies our growth and our freedom."

In every thought, there is a feeling, an emotion. Either that thought comes from your true self, the *observer*, or it is a conditioned response that is stored in your subconscious mind. You can know its origin by just asking yourself this: "If I had the choice to discontinue this thought, would I take it?" Everything we do is for the reward experienced by the emotion, the feeling of happiness. Whether it is for a thing, an outcome, a relationship, more money, or something else, the core motivation is to experience the emotion of bliss, of happiness.

Many years ago I found myself like everyone else

living a life that was very stressful. The business I owned was quite successful, but that success brought with it a lot of demands on me and my time. I was always up against deadlines, and I was constantly being pulled in many directions. My skills were unique, which meant I was the go-to person when things weren't working. I was usually solving somebody's last-minute crisis. The business afforded me the income to have and do all the things that I had always wanted to do. I had a beautiful recording studio to explore my musical ideas; through a lot of expensive instruction, I had become a single-digit handicapper in golf; I had six figures tied up in woodworking machinery, which was a real dream come true for a lifelong woodworker; and I had a pilot's license, something I had wanted since childhood. Ironically, though, I had no time to enjoy any of it. I was basically owned by my business, not the other way around.

One night I had an experience that I can only describe as an epiphany. I was lying in bed staring at where the wall meets the ceiling. There was just enough ambient light for my eyes to make that intersection of planes visible, and for some reason I was focused on it. The rest of the family was fast asleep, but my racing mind was filled with emotional responses as it contemplated everything I had on my plate. How much time would that job take? Could I get across town on time for that meeting tomorrow afternoon? How did my schedule get so jammed?

I'm not sure why this particular thought came into

my head, but it occurred to me in the midst of this mental mayhem that if I could just stop thinking, if I could just stop having thoughts, all of this inner turmoil would go away. As I mention earlier, thought is the vehicle of emotion, and no thinking means no thoughts. And at that moment all of my thoughts were stress-related. The only emotion I was feeling was anxiety.

What made this experience so different was that it was not an intellectual exercise. Anyone could have said those words to me. Of course, it makes sense. But this was very different. This was an experience that was happening to me. I felt a conscious knowing, or what people in many spiritual circles call a download. In the midst of this contemplative moment, something opened up inside of me. When that happened, there was nothing to understand and nothing to figure out. I just knew this truth and surrendered to it completely, without resistance. I didn't have to try to do anything. In fact, I wasn't in control of it.

The experience created an immediate sense of silence in my mind, a complete sense of stillness, no extraneous thinking, just a total immersion in the present moment, one that I can't articulate. I felt an all-encompassing sense of peace and calmness descend on me. This is sometimes referred to as bliss, meaning I was happy for no particular reason at all. That's the best kind of happiness, and it was even more pronounced because it was juxtaposed with how I had been feeling just minutes before. The anxiety that had been so pervasive simultaneously disappeared, and it all transpired in a microsecond. I felt no need to question it. I was just completely absorbed in a total sense of relief in light of all the anxiety that I had been wrestling with just moments before.

I fell asleep shortly after that, probably because my body was so exhausted from the constant fight-or-flight hormones flooding it. I didn't stir for the rest of the night. When I woke up the next morning, the total sense of relief and bliss was still with me, but I still felt no need to question it. I thought, "Well, of course this is true. It's so obvious. My thoughts and my emotions are inseparable. If I control my thoughts, I control my emotions." More importantly, I understood that if my mind is quiet, if I have no thoughts, I cannot experience stress because the emotion of stress needs the process of thinking in order to communicate that feeling. Why didn't I just do this a long time ago and save myself all the grief? That's when I knew something had changed in me. I'm not really sure what to call it, perhaps an awakening. The intensity of the experience remained with me for days after that. I floated through life with complete impunity toward stressful situations. That truth is still with me so many years later. I'm not sure whether the intensity has softened or whether it has just become more of who I am, but the experience feels normal.

However, the experience has made me much more aware of how other people handle stress. People often catastrophize situations even though intellectually they may understand that their reaction only makes the situation feel worse. The energy they expend in their reaction is exhausting, and it offers no traction toward a positive resolution of the problem. People can seem powerless to respond differently, perhaps because they don't realize where their reaction is coming from or how to stop it. They assume it is just their emotions, and "you can't control your emotions."

I once read a story about a woman with serious illnesses having a conversation with an Indian yogi. The woman told the yogi all her health problems, and the yogi listened with compassion but didn't seem to be upset. The woman felt confused and even a little annoyed at his lack of emotion, so she asked him, "Don't you have any problems in your life?" He told her that in his life nothing ever went wrong. As he explained, there is no point worrying about things you can control because you can control them. It also makes no sense to worry about things you can't control because you can't control them. That covers everything, doesn't it? This story brought a light-hearted smile to my face. It is such a simple truism, but it described what I was experiencing, a complete surrender to a totally practical perspective that cannot be disputed.

As for this chapter's main question, "Are you thinking or being thought?" the answer isn't one many people like. While we have the ability to be the thinker of all of our thoughts, scientific research confirms that at least 95 percent of the time we are being thought. As I mentioned, we have been installing programs into our subconscious mind our entire life. Those programs are like computer files ready to be executed. When a certain stimulus occurs, our subconscious goes and gets what it thinks is the appropriate file for the response and runs it. We experience the thought response from the thinking we have previously installed. We then immediately experience the emotional content that goes along with it. When that happens, our blood chemistry changes to reflect our emotional response. However, before going further, I should clarify that we have one mind. When we use labels such as *conscious mind*, *subconscious mind*, *unconscious mind*, and so on, we are speaking about different aspects of one entity. Not only do we have only one mind, quantum physics tells us that we are all connected and part of *one* mind. Our five senses just don't have the ability to decode the information to make that obvious.

That's really not difficult to understand. There are lots of sounds that our ears are incapable of hearing because the frequency is beyond the range of human hearing. There are light frequencies, such as ultraviolet or infrared, that we cannot see. These were totally unknown until we developed the technology to make them visible. Stand outside and look at the night sky. The number of stars we can see is a fraction of the billions we can't see because our eyes are not powerful enough. Not even binoculars can help us see all of them. Dogs can pick up scents that are right in front of our noses, and yet we don't smell them.

That being said, our sensory awareness seems limited for a necessary reason. Our subconscious mind is literally ten times faster than our conscious mind. We wouldn't survive for very long if that weren't the case. When something unexpected happens, such as tripping while walking, we don't have to figure out how to keep our balance. If we touch something really hot, we don't need to stand there thinking, "Hmm, what should I do next?" Our subconscious has that program, and it acts instantly to keep us from being burned without our intervention (or our choice). We don't have to learn how to walk every time we stand up. We don't have to learn how to button our shirt, tie our shoes, swallow our food, or any other physical aspect of our daily routine.

We also don't have to learn how to react to a stressful situation or an annoying person. Unless we want to *change* that response, we already have at least one installed, and it's waiting to step in and be executed simply by observing the corresponding stimulus. A close friend once told me about how they always reacted in a certain way to a situation, and their reaction made them feel badly about themself. I said, "Well, you are really good at that reaction because you have repeated it so many times. You have practiced it over and over again, like a musical scale. That is why it is effortless and it flows so easily. You have fully mastered it." That is why replacing that same reaction with something different can feel so difficult. In order to install a new reaction, we have to practice new mechanics. While we are doing that, the response we have mastered will no doubt push back against the new one. This is not a bad thing. It's just the system, and it can work for us as easily as against our desires. It only feels like a bad way of functioning when we want to *change* a behavior. From another perspective, if we tend to be really calm in a situation that sets other people off, that detached calmness is also our mastered response, and it would take perhaps prolonged pressure for a different response to break through.

Our subconscious mind catalogs and stores all kinds of information so that it can be recalled instantly, in microseconds. In fact, it's largely believed that during the first seven years of life, our basic personality is formed. This is very important to understand as it pertains to parenting but also to understanding why we are who we are today. In the first seven years of life, our brain waves are basically a hypnotized sponge observing what is going on. How do people react to stress? How do they talk? How do they treat other people when they are happy, sad, or angry? We learn during this time how to fit into the "tribe" that we have been born into. From my perspective, this is no different than herd animals like gazelles, who must learn very quickly how to fit into the herd and what to do in order to survive. Newborn gazelles must learn what to be afraid of and when to feel safe, when to run, and so on. They do this mostly through observation. That's how we learn so much in the beginning, before we can speak.

I was doing service work in an elementary school when the principal asked me to take a ride with him to another building to assess a piano and decide whether it should be replaced. During the ride, he shared a story about a young child they were having problems with. The child used completely inappropriate language, and speaking with the child had proved pointless. The principal visited the child's home to speak with his parents. When the father answered the door, the principal explained why he was there. I'm guessing you know where this is going. The father delivered a string of inappropriate words as he told the principal to mind his own business. The child was merely parroting the behaviors he was observing.

Here's another example. One day I was spending time with my grandson, who was about eighteen months old. We were rolling a toy truck back and forth on the kitchen floor, and I noticed that he would pick up the truck from wherever it had stopped, return it to where I was, and then strike a very distinctive pose: kneeling on one knee with his arm resting on the other knee, as if he were a player on the sideline waiting to be sent into the game. Each time he did this, he looked directly at me. Initially, I thought it was quite curious. I couldn't figure out why he was doing it until I realized that I was in that position. He was imitating me. My daughter later told me that, after I left that day, he continued that behavior for days even though it was not being reinforced by my presence. Imagine how constant exposure to any behavior installs that predisposition.

From my perspective, it was fascinating how even during the distraction of playing with the truck, my grandson's subconscious mind was watching his environment and taking notes.

Similarly, when my daughter drops something by accident, she often says, "Oh my," and then picks it up. Before long, my eighteen-month-old grandson was doing the same thing: If he dropped something, or if he saw someone else drop something, he would volunteer an "oh my" and deliver it with the same tone and inflection as his mother. As you can see, this programming can be very powerful or very damaging. In my opinion, we should ask ourselves: "What programming am I offering and what programming am I watching and therefore installing into my own subconscious?" To play off of the chapter title, we could ask, "Am I the programmer of myself, or am I the one being programmed?" Do we even know?

Because of this, you must work at what I call *thought awareness training* (which I discuss in my previous books, *The Practicing Mind* and *Fully Engaged*). You cannot change any behavior, any response or reaction, if you are not aware you are doing it. This is no truer than it is in the realm of *thinking*. If you are not aware of what thoughts your mind is producing, then your mind is operating without your permission. You can't change the programming that is running if you are totally immersed in the experience of the programs. If you do not have awareness and at least some level of control over what your mind is doing, then you have no real power in your life. You are capable of being manipulated either by someone else or by your own unconscious and the inadvertent programming that you have installed. Without thought awareness, you don't have the privilege of choice, the opportunity to evaluate what programming is working, what programming needs to be erased, and what new programming needs to be installed. Over and over again I observe people who are complete prisoners of their minds rather than masters who use their minds to create emotional freedom from stress, to conquer impatience and lack of focus to achieve what is so important to them. This may sound like an oversimplification, but what we're talking about is just a skill. Everything we do in life can be distilled down to a skill, and as I state, the more we practice the skills we want with conscious intention, the more effortless they become and the more freedom we experience.

To me, the game of golf offers an excellent example for understanding how our minds work. Unlike most sports, golf is not reactionary. Unlike tennis or baseball, in which the ball comes at the player and forces them to react, a golf ball just sits there waiting to be hit. It will wait forever. This gives the mind lots of time to think, which actually interferes with performance. Golf is mostly a battle between you, your thinking mind, and who is in control at that moment. Because a golfer's ability to perform consistently at their highest level depends on this back-and-forth mental dialogue, a lot of research has been conducted to understand this relationship between the player and their mind.

One thing researchers understand very well is the difference between focusing on your golf swing and simply golfing. The unskilled player is typically immersed in their swing mechanics. They are at times almost paralyzed by trying to consciously remember all the different body positions they have to move through to execute a sound golf swing. This doesn't work very well and usually leads to frustration, since the effort itself often undermines the goal of getting the ball up in the air and hopefully advancing in the desired direction. However, once a player has practiced their swing mechanics to a point of repletion, the conscious mind reaches a point where it stops thinking through the golf swing, and the swing just happens. Before a player can excel, they must first dissolve the technical barriers. This is true not only in golf but in any difficult experience in life.

When this point is reached, the golfer *experiences* the whole course. They see the shape of the fairways, the hazards, and the undulations of the greens as inviting challenges, and their skill allows them the freedom to create a particular strategy to meet those challenges and to execute it. They hit the ball high, they hit the ball low, and they curve it to the right or left as their creative mind sees it. This point of mastery, which can only be obtained by understanding the fundamentals and practicing them till they become part of you, allows the player to experience a round of golf in ways that those unwilling to put in the time and effort cannot imagine. That freedom awaits you in life.

CHAPTER 3

Interpretation Creates Experience

Repeat This Mantra

If you learn just one thing from reading this book, the mantra "interpretation creates experience" would be the most important in my opinion. It might not seem believable at first, but as Viktor Frankl said, in every situation we get to choose our reaction. So our interpretation of whatever is happening in front of us is what creates our experience of that situation. I hammer this into all of the people that I work with.

Where does your interpretation come from? What data goes into forming it? Well, almost always it comes from programming. The catch-22 regarding programming is that it creates and perpetuates "like" programming. If a certain situation arises and you react to it based on a response that is installed in your subconscious, your reaction will act as a practice session anchoring your response even more strongly. This is how we habitualize the way that we think and react to situations. It's how we create our perception of the world in general. When we step back and look at it from outside of a particular emotional response, it's a beautiful system. We just misuse it because we're unaware that we are participating in it. When we understand that this is going on every minute of every day, we give ourselves the opportunity to change the programming and thus the response and the experience itself. We have the power to experience life as we would like. Science tells us that. However, this is not so easy because any habitual response we have created has tremendous strength. When it's working for us, it's a huge asset, but when it's working against us, we'd better have a plan to deal with it.

I was once working with a brilliant young man who was struggling with a lack of self-confidence and constant self-doubt. His interpretation of any particular situation was usually "what could go wrong will go wrong." At the time he was badly in need of employment. During one conversation, he commented that there was a company that he would really like to work for. He had a friend who was employed there, and he was pretty sure that his friend could get him an interview. However, he struggled with whether to ask him for his influence and intervention because he felt he would be taking advantage of his friend. He was very conflicted. I told him that his dilemma was coming not from the situation itself but from his interpretation of the situation. He asked me how, since he didn't see any other way to experience it. I told him that any interview is two-sided. The employer needs to decide if a person is right for the job, and it's the person's responsibility to decide if the employer is someone they feel is deserving of their knowledge and skills. I knew this man to be extremely intelligent and very knowledgeable about the subject matter of this job. He had unique qualities that perhaps no one else working at this company possessed. He could certainly offer suggestions that were unique to his experience and possible solutions to problems that no one else might have. But if he didn't sit down and speak with the employer, they would never be aware that he and his talents were even available.

This situation was very close to me. Many years ago, when I was a high-level concert piano technician and working with many notable celebrities, the CEO of a performing arts center that I worked for told me that he was surprised I didn't advertise anywhere that I was their technician. I responded that I felt it might sound like I was blowing my horn, and I didn't want to come off that way. He said, "Well, that is one way of looking at it. However, if I knew that I had access to the same technician that was working for these famous world-class musicians, and that he would gladly come to my home and do work for me, I would want to know that." That was his interpretation. I had never looked at it from that perspective. After hearing it, I felt almost obligated to share those credentials in my promotions. It was a 180-degree swing in perspective. The situation was just the situation, but the interpretation defined how it was experienced.

As for the young man, I also reminded him that everyone else in this situation could make their own choices: His friend might say, "No, I would be uncomfortable doing that," or he might say, "Absolutely, you would be perfect for the job." The employer might say, "No, we are not interested in interviewing him." The situation had many possibilities and could unfold in numerous ways, but none of those outcomes were available if he didn't allow himself to explore it. If he was in fact interviewed for the job, the employer might be so impressed with him that they would thank his friend for the referral, which could place his friend in a favorable position. Just like me, the young man responded that he had never thought of the situation from that perspective. So I stressed the point with him to be the observer of his interpretation because it was the driver of his experience.

In general, most experiences are not one thing or another. They are not absolute. We interpret situations based on our past experiences and the programming we have installed. We do this millions of times throughout our lives, and so functioning in this way feels normal. We feel we are present and are the one in charge of it all. Except in moments when we are mindful, we do not view a situation from the nonjudgmental perspective of "I have a choice here, so where do I want this to go and what is my plan to get there?" More than likely, when someone says something we like, we feel good, and when they say something we don't like, we feel bad or irritated.

The truth is that we are not always in control of what happens *to* us. We are, however, *always* in control of how we respond, or at least we have that opportunity if we realize that it exists and we work at giving it to ourselves. Just because we may be so wrapped up in the emotional content of the moment that we don't take advantage of that choice doesn't mean it doesn't exist. Our interpretation, whether inspiring or upsetting, becomes the stimulus that pulls the trigger and tells our subconscious mind which file to run. At that point, we either intervene or go along for the ride.

How do we escape this modality? Well, this reoccurring phenomenon cannot be viewed from the perspective of being in our thoughts, in the interpretation itself. We must be the *observer*, our true self, who we really are, the one outside of the thinking mind. In Eastern thought systems, there is a saying: "I use my emotions; I don't allow my emotions to use me." This truth is ancient. Our thoughts are always creating our reality whether we are aware of it or not. We are only truly free when our thoughts are deliberate and coming from *our* will. Otherwise, our behavior is just a trigger waiting to be pulled either by something someone says or by a circumstance that arises.

A corporate executive confided in me that when he was called into meetings, he would listen to others speak but not offer his own suggestions or comments. He remained quiet because he was afraid that if he spoke up he might say something others might think was irrelevant or uninformed, which would make him feel foolish. These meetings were comprised of people from many levels in the company. Some individuals were much higher up the ladder than him, and he didn't want to say something that revealed he was unaware of something that should be common knowledge. He was also concerned about finding the right words to express himself. He said that when he was in a stressful situation his mind would drop words, and he would start to hesitate as he tried to articulate his ideas.

I told him he was making assumptions with no data. If his perspective had no value, then presumably he wouldn't have been asked to attend the meeting. He may not be the CEO, but his position in the company and his experience had earned him the right to be present. His interpretation gave him an internal justification to stay silent — that it was better to be unnoticed than noticed for the wrong reason. However, my interpretation was that he could just as easily share something useful, such as a perspective that no one else had thought of, something that a more senior employee might consider quite insightful and a valuable contribution. Since not everyone was involved in the everyday minutiae in his department, some were probably unaware of any particular situation and might appreciate his input. I told him that when we are feeling fearful and doubting ourselves, that fear *isn't* who *we* are. It's just a thought playing out, and we are *in* it rather than watching it.

This is just a fraction of the amazing power you give yourself by the simple act of spending just ten minutes a day practicing thought awareness training. *The daily repetition of this act* will open the door and allow you to step outside the prison of being ruled by unintentional programming. This is one of those things that bears repeating: You cannot change what you are unaware of. Awareness must come first before you can afford yourself the privilege of choice in the matter. You can't be in the play and directing it at the same time. I want you to have the experience I described of the night when it occurred to me that if I didn't think, I wouldn't feel stress. What I was consciously realizing on a deep level was that I am not my thoughts. I exist outside of most of the thoughts I experience (unless I am deliberately creating them). Therefore, being independent, I have the opportunity to become aware of and to control that process for my own happiness. I want that truth to be a fundamental, core part of your perspective. I want you to feel that a daily practice that builds that skill is just as much a necessary part of your routine as eating and sleeping. You must nourish that faculty so that it becomes stronger and a natural part of how you operate.

For about two weeks, my corporate client dutifully practiced thought awareness training, and the next time I spoke with him, he was elated. As he shared with me his experience of a meeting he attended earlier in the week, he was somewhat taken aback. Here is what he described:

Tom, it was the strangest feeling. I found myself sitting there listening to one of the higher-ups speak. While listening, I decided that I wanted to volunteer some information that I felt was pertinent to the subject being discussed. I "noticed" my usual response of fear, but my experience in that moment was that I was sitting next to myself and not actually that person. I was observing that thought response almost like listening to an audio file being played, but I knew it wasn't me. It was just a file being played. It could have just as easily been playing for someone else. The feeling was surreal. Because of that I felt no fear in speaking up and adding my comments. I was stunned when the CEO said exactly what you predicted might be possible. He was impressed with my observations and said they were very valuable information for him to consider and wondered why no one had thought of it before. When I spoke, "I" was completely calm. There was no hesitation in my thoughts and I had total clarity expressing myself. It was a game changer for me moving forward.

Electricity has always been available to us. For thousands of years, it was waiting to be harnessed so it could serve us. We just didn't know that it existed until recent history. Before that, people sat in the dim light of candles. Understanding the relationship between the real you and the different aspects of your mind is like learning the skill of reading. If you cannot read, you are denied access to so much information and to the freedom and power that that information gives you.

Everything that I am talking about in this book I live every day. I have used all that I have written about for years, and I feel it is important to say that one of the problems with being a communicator of information like this can be that people assume that you are always able to execute it flawlessly. That simply isn't true. I remember one afternoon when one of my daughters had stopped by my house and was sitting at the kitchen table talking with me. For some reason, I got on a rant about something that I found frustrating and annoying. She patiently listened, and then with a slight smile on her face, she slid in front of me a copy of one of my books that, as fate would have it, was on the kitchen table. She then calmly said, "I think you need to read chapter two again." What can I say? I am not always on my game. No one is. I think people some-times make the mistake of assuming that when you're re-ally knowledgeable about a subject like this, and you are a successful communicator of information, you are always executing the process at the highest level, and that's not the case.

If there is a difference in my experience versus some-one else's, it's that I don't get upset with myself regarding my performance level when it fluctuates from day to day because I'm aware that this is a lifetime practice. It is part of the process of creating a happy and healthy life, and you are always up against the threshold of your skill level. We don't notice when things are easy because we are good at them and they feel effortless. We notice when our lack of skill pushes back against us, but that is the sensation of normal growth. There is no room for judging performance. I can't say it's not productive because it does produce results. They just tend to make us feel bad. I won't say that I don't analyze my performance at times. But in my opinion, judging is usually a comparison between where I am at the moment and my best performance, which is what we will cover in the next chapter.

CHAPTER 4

When You Get Better Than You Are

Understanding Your Scoring Barriers

Over the past eighteen years of working with people of all ages and backgrounds, I have had the opportunity to experience many different personalities and their typical struggles, which people usually feel are unique to them. But from my vantage point, they are not. The struggles that we think are known only to us are present in everyone's life, just in different disguises. This is another understanding that needs to be repeated often because it can completely change our experience of any particular moment.

What is a scoring barrier? A scoring barrier is a perceived limitation in our abilities. It can manifest in any area of life. It can be anything, from beating a certain personal-best time in a marathon to earning a certain income. In general, we aren't aware of scoring barriers consciously. They're pretty sneaky and can covertly sabotage our efforts when we get close to them. I think they work in two different ways. One way is that they impact our performance capabilities when we exceed what we are used to. The other way they manifest, ironically, is almost the opposite. We keep getting more or improve, but we feel like we have or can do less. That creates its own feeling of a barrier that we can't get past. They are both rooted in our urge to reach perfection.

What is your definition of perfection? I think everyone experiences a sense of incompleteness, one we become aware of in contemplative moments. We are always searching for that something we believe is going to make that feeling of incompleteness finally stop. That feeling is a major component of how we are manipulated by marketing media. The core subliminal message behind marketing serves to nurture the feeling that we can't be happy with who we are and where we are right now. We need that new item, that experience, or that change, and so on, and then we will finally be happy. We will finally get relief from that nagging sense of "I'm almost happy but not quite." Regardless of how hard we work and how many goals we reach, that feeling never goes away, does it? There is an old saying that the people who worry about money the most are the people who have a lot and the people who have very little.

Five years ago I was asked by the CEO of a growing company to do a presentation at an annual conference. This began a friendly relationship with this person, and over time I've been privy to the company's financial growth.

When I first met the CEO, the company was earning $750,000 a year. This number allowed the company to pay its employees a fair salary and to afford the CEO a very comfortable income. He and his family had a very nice home in an expensive neighborhood, they belonged to an upscale country club, and his family of four traveled the world flying first class and staying in five-star hotels.

His goal was to break the seven-figure barrier. That represented a level of success he coveted. The following year the company reached just over $2 million in revenue. Within the next year, they were up around $7 million in revenue. After a few more years, they were heading for over $20 million in yearly revenue with only a few new employees to add to the payroll.

I asked him, "How will you feel if next year you only make $15 million?" He was silent. I told him I remembered when he said he had everything he wanted for himself and his family when the company wasn't even making a million dollars. I said, "I'm curious, if your income stays the same or even goes down, will you feel like a failure even though you are a multimillionaire and have more money than you need?" After an awkward silence, I said, "You don't need to answer. It's just something for you to think about for your own sense of perspective."

A trap we can all fall into is the addiction to having more. The problem with "more" is that what was more yesterday when we didn't have it is no longer more once we have it. More is continually redefined as what we don't have. It can be an all-consuming obsession with no end to the hunger. There is a difference between having more stuff and increasing our personal growth. Ironically, I usually find that the more evolved someone is from a personal growth perspective, the less importance they place on stuff. Their definition of perfection and the perfect life can be very different when compared to those addicted to more.

From my perspective, *perfection* is not a state that we finally reach, at least not in this lifetime. It's not a certain amount of money, a certain number of possessions, or a certain level of skill in an art form. All of these are limitations in one form or another. Any *place* or finite number we try to "get to" is limited by nature. During my tenure as a concert piano technician, I spent quite a bit of time working with some of the best artists and musicians the world has ever seen. Besides musicians, I also worked extensively with dance and ballet companies from around the world. I can tell you that none of them felt that they were as good as they could be. None of them even put effort into thinking about such a thing because they knew their art form was infinite, and that was something they cherished. True perfection is the ability to expand infinitely; it must be endless in nature.

In Richard Bach's great book *Jonathan Livingston Seagull*, there is a scene after Jonathan has passed away, and he finds himself on a beach training in flight maneuvers that are quite a bit above the ones he left behind on earth. He is perplexed by the fact that there don't seem to be very many other seagulls on the beach learning to fly as he is. So he asks his instructor, Chiang, if this is heaven. Chiang replies, "You are a very fast flier, aren't you?" Jonathan is taken aback and very pleased that his instructor has noticed his skill. Chiang says, "You will begin to touch heaven, Jonathan, in the moment that you touch perfect speed. And that isn't flying a thousand miles an hour, or a million, or flying at the speed of light. Because any number is a limit, and perfection doesn't have limits. Perfect speed, my son, is being there." And with that Chiang disappears and reappears several hundred yards down the beach and then disappears and reappears next to Jonathan. The story is a metaphor, and what Chiang is trying to teach Jonathan is that despite all his efforts to go faster, there is no speed he will reach that will fulfill his desire to reach perfect speed because it is not a number. Any number would be a limit. Jonathan is infinite in his ability to grow, to expand and to know no limits. This truth can be interpreted as either a blessing in its endless offerings or as a constant reminder that "ugh, I'm not there yet."

That is what the feeling of incompleteness is really telling us. It is what drives us as human spirits to grow. Without it we would have no motivation, no excitement in becoming more of who we can be. When we stop using and misinterpreting that feeling to be something negative, our experience changes immensely. All it takes sometimes is a simple shift in perspective to reveal that truth.

I once mentored a female college athlete who struggled with self-criticism. She was in a team sport, and when she didn't play well, she was so hard on herself that her negative behavior toward herself was a distraction to her teammates. It got to a point where the coach confronted her and told her to either fix it or get off the team. When she came to me, she was going into her junior year. I asked her at what age she had started playing, and she said the third grade. I asked her if she was better now than in the third grade, and she answered, "Of course I am." I then asked her if she was better now than when she was a senior in high school, and of course she said yes. I had noticed she was self-critical whenever she compared herself to upper-class players on the team, so I asked, "Are there freshman on the team, girls just out of high school?" She said yes. I asked, "How do you think a first-year freshman sitting on the bench and wanting to be put into the game feels about you when she watches you play? Do you think she is at least a little bit intimidated? You have played two entire seasons as a college athlete in your sport. You have two years more of practice and game experience than she does. Is it fair for her to expect to play at your level?"

Predictably, she responded, "Well, no, it isn't. I never thought of it that way. When I think of it from that perspective, I guess that's what I'm doing and it doesn't make much sense." Then I asked her if she thought that next season she would be better than the past season, and if there would ever come a point when she wouldn't be able to get any better. At that point, if it came, wouldn't she probably quit, since the game would get pretty boring?

In sports as in life, no one has their A game all day every day. My jazz piano instructor, whose skill level was off the charts, said that the reason we practice is so that our worst performance is acceptable. We should always try to focus on that instead of judging each moment of our daily performance against our best.

I'm happy to say that the brief discussion changed this young woman's experience of how she viewed her journey as an athlete and how she participated in the sport. All I really did was pull her out of the loop of behavior that she had installed over several decades. Just for a moment, she became the *observer* of what programs she was allowing to play out. We then came up with a plan to help her push back against her well-practiced responses to less-than-perfect play, which would undoubtedly show up again.

Scoring barriers don't just refer to performance numbers, such as a score in sports. They refer to barriers created by our interpretations. The first conscious experience I had with a scoring barrier was early in my golf instruction when I was trying to break into the seventies. I could almost get there, but right when I thought it was going to happen, I would have a bad hole and ruin my chances. Eric MacCluen, the PGA teaching pro that I was working with, gave me some commonsense clarity on the situation. I told him that I was always hovering around eighty or eighty-one, and I couldn't seem to push through into the seventies. He asked me how many times I played a week, and I told him once. He said, "Well, that's the problem." I didn't understand why, since though I only played once a week, I practiced a lot. He explained that if someone only plays once, they only have one chance a week to break their scoring barrier. That puts a tremendous amount of pressure on that one game, since if the person doesn't do it that day, they'll have to wait a whole week before trying again. On the other hand, if someone plays five times a week, each game is no big deal. If they don't reach their score one day, they'll be back out again the next day and the day after that. By adopting that perspective, it would drop the self-imposed pressure, and the player would relax and probably perform better. In other words, if I changed my interpretation, I would have a different experience. That turned out to be correct.

This helped me understand how scoring barriers work psychologically. As this chapter shows, they influence a whole lot more than just a golf score, but sports are a good analogy for seeing how they work. For instance, at one time, my scoring barrier was ninety, and I experienced all the same things I did when trying to break eighty. We unconsciously install into our subconscious reactions to our performance in any situation that let us know that we are functioning at our current skill level. We are comfortable playing at that level. And when we begin to get close to our personal-best performance level, our scoring barrier, we start to get uneasy. We can feel like, "I'm not this good; something is going to go wrong." We might not consciously say this to ourselves, but the *feeling* is there.

I definitely experienced this in my golf game, and I know it is not unusual. When it happens, we are basically unintentionally instructing our subconscious mind to go get the programming that will produce the result that will bring us back into our comfort zone. It obeys our wishes, and we totally implode. Once we realize that we are no longer up against our scoring barrier, we relax because we are now performing at a level that we *know* we can sustain. With this, our playing skills magically return because we are back in familiar territory internally. I have watched this phenomenon happen to other golfers many times. I once played with a guy who, according to him, was having his best round ever. He commented, "I don't know what's going on. I have never played this well. I hope I don't screw up and mess up my score." When he said that, I knew he had just sabotaged his game, and on the very next hole, a completely different player showed up. After he had totally ruined his score for the round, his swing magically showed up again.

It is very important to understand this process if you want to be in control of it. If you are aware of your thoughts, you can notice when this phenomenon is beginning. That gives you the opportunity to choose the feeling that will nurture the performance that you are experiencing. That is when you must be a deliberate thinker, not the one being thought. Above, what my golfing partner wasn't seeing was that he obviously had the ability to perform at a higher level when he didn't get in his own way mentally. We can't be better than we are. We can only limit our potential. For him, his skill level only dropped when he began to question it.

Over and over again, I tell those I am mentoring that thought awareness is the key to the prison door. It's the engine that runs personal change. The deliberate thinker lives the mantra: "I am not my thoughts. I use my thoughts. I don't allow my thoughts to use me." As for the golfer, his lack of awareness that he was not his thoughts sealed his fate. His game imploded for several holes until he reached a scoring level he felt he was capable of, and then magically his swing fell back into place and his ability returned to his normal skill level.

CHAPTER 5

What Is Struggle Really Telling You?

Moving to the Other Side of Fear

I have a saying: "The truth is the truth whether or not you know about it, whether or not you agree with it, or whether or not you believe it." When Galileo was jailed for stating that the earth was not the center of the universe, he was speaking the truth. But many, if not most, of his contemporaries did not know that he was speaking the truth. They didn't agree with it or believe it, but it was still the truth. As I mention in the introduction, for centuries, people in the East reached states of mind that Westerners often considered paranormal. Many who did not possess their commitment to practicing meditation had never experienced what the monks experienced daily, and so they did not believe them. Now our science can show their heightened brain activity on a screen.

We create our reality in every moment by the thoughts that we have and by our interpretation of those thoughts. That is the truth whether we are aware of it or not. It is the truth whether we are aware that we are doing it or not. It is the truth regardless of whether we think it is fair, whether we take control of it, and whether we commit to mastering that skill. If you are not in control of your thinking the majority of the time, if you are not *deliberate* in your thinking, then you are not in control of what you feel or what shows up in your life, and your ability to realize your potential is limited by default. In *The Practicing Mind*, I used the analogy of the chariot rider who is not holding the reins and therefore is an involuntary participant on the ride. The rider is not guiding the horses, which represent the energy of our thinking down *our* directed path. The horses are just running full out over the rough terrain and constantly changing direction depending on which horse is more in control at the moment. I'm sure there are moments in your life where you feel like this. We all experience them.

When you are in a situation, any situation, there will be an internal reaction. So ask yourself: "What will that reaction be? More importantly, what *can* that reaction be?" Your subconscious can only go get what is already there *unless* you are in the process of creating new programming. As I mention earlier, people have always wanted to fly, and they only failed because they didn't understand the mechanics of flight. Similarly, we have always wanted to be more in control of what we experience and less of a victim. Just like how Bernoulli's principle brought the freedom to realize flight, our ever-increasing understanding of where our behaviors come from brings us the freedom to change those behaviors. We are not our behaviors! I will say that again: We are not our behaviors. We execute behaviors that we have learned and practiced and at present may have little control over, but these can be replaced. This is a very important concept to take in. A psychologist friend of mine once told me that it is very difficult to reach people with behavioral issues because they mistake their behaviors for who they are. In other words, if you constructively criticize their behavior, they interpret it as if you are attacking their self-worth. They become defensive and shut down to communication. I think we are all susceptible to this at one time or another, even when we are trying to be on our guard. Our subconscious response to a critical comment is so incredibly fast that we find ourselves reacting in a way we did not consciously choose. At that point we are deep in the emotion of our reaction and that can be very difficult to overcome.

Changing our behaviors requires knowledge of where we are, where we want to be, and how to get there. It requires practice, which means repeating deliberate responses to situations, responses that have been consciously calculated to bring about the change in experience we are looking for. This all takes effort. We can interpret that effort in different ways, which will directly impact our experience of exerting the effort.

Here is another truth I will repeat and that I want you to keep close to your heart: Everything in life is a skill. It doesn't matter whether it's learning to walk, learning to feed yourself, learning to conduct an interview, or learning how to have a successful relationship. They are all skills. With all skills, we start from the beginning, which is a place of no skill. We then move along the line of skill development. We call that learning. So what is your interpretation of the process of learning, whatever skill you are working on? I've always found it curious how we attach judgment to particular words; for example, the word *mistake*. The word *mistake* conjures up an uncomfortable feeling, a sense of doing wrong, of failing, of perhaps being inadequate. In reality, the word refers to a process of data-gathering. It is a natural part of learning what works and what doesn't work. Yes, some mistakes carry more weight than others, but I'm not speaking about mistakes that could cost people their lives, although even in those situations, we learn a hard lesson of what works and what doesn't work. I think it's safe to say that in everyday life, the mistakes we make are honest mistakes and don't come from intentionally doing something wrong, and yet when we make these mistakes, they tend to make us feel bad about ourselves. There is a certain subliminal sense of fear with regard to mistakes. What will others think of us if we make a mistake? This is another example of how our interpretations create our experience.

The word *struggle* also deserves some examination. At first glance the word *struggle* conjures up a sense of difficulty. But both of these words, *struggle* and *difficulty*, refer to a *feeling* that we experience. That is the interpretation and it is not absolute. Some people would feel a sense of struggle to give a speech in front of hundreds of people. Other people would look forward to it. I have observed an early-childhood teacher go through mornings in a room full of out-of-control five-year-olds, each demanding attention, with total calmness on her face and a sense of enjoyment. Most of us would *struggle* and find it *difficult* to get through those mornings. So what is driving the difference in experience? It's the interpretation. But what is driving the interpretation? The level of skill of the participant. In other words, our interpretation of this experience would be based on our relative mastery of this particular skill.

When you're in a situation that is creating a sense of struggle, what that is really telling you is that you are in the process of mastering that particular situation. If you had already mastered it, you would already be good at it, and you probably wouldn't notice it because it would be effortless. The key here is that we don't have to judge that feeling of struggle as being bad. We can interpret it as an awareness that we are in the process of developing our skill in this particular activity. When I work with people, I ask them, "If you could be really good at dealing with this particular situation, would you like to be? Would you like to be so good at it that you experience that inspirational feeling that comes from mastering something that used to be difficult?" Quite predictably they answer yes. And

I tell them that to get from where they are now to where they want to be requires being in the circumstances that demand the skill. That is when you have the opportunity to execute your practice plan. In fact, it's the only time that you can really get an accurate read on where you are in the skill. When interpreted from this perspective, that feeling of struggle or difficulty is judged to be "this is what I've been waiting for," and your experience becomes very different.

One important technique for refining your interpretations of a situation is to monitor your feelings. In the beginning of practicing to consciously intervene in your interpretation of a situation, it is too difficult to stay out in front of your preprogrammed thinking, but your *feelings* are more in your face. They are a better heads-up as to when you need to pull back and analyze where your interpretation is taking you.

I think that we have unknowingly predefined the feeling of struggle or difficulty as having a component of fear. That fear is coming from the reaction that you have told yourself you should have to this particular situation. You can burn the energy of that fear by using it as the fuel to develop the skill. In other words, you use the energy that you are wasting on worrying and apply it to the process of what you're going through in whatever way you can. Perhaps that means trying to understand why you feel the way you do about the particular situation, checking in with yourself, and asking what is the worst that could happen. I find that many times when I ask someone what is the worst that can happen, it pulls them out of the behavioral reaction of fear long enough for them to see the situation from a different perspective. That brief moment allows them the opportunity to have a different interpretation.

If you are aware of what thoughts your mind is producing, you have the ability to see these feelings of struggle or difficulty as messengers alerting you to the opportunity present before you. The most important part of the process of change when dealing with all of this is to remember the phrase I coined: "do, observe, correct," or DOC. When faced with an opportunity to execute changes in your interpretation, practice your plan. That is the "do" portion. Understand that that portion will always be limited to where you are in the development of that skill. We don't get angry at a child in the second grade because they can't do higher math. They aren't there yet, and that is normal. Treat yourself the same way. You're on a path of change to a more powerful you. Execute your plan for the situation, and then "observe" how it impacts your experience without judgment. You can and should analyze what happened, but avoid judging what you observe as good or bad. Judging can be infused with undesirable emotions, which can work against you. Analysis has a more detached perspective. Afterward, make your "correction" for the next round. It's a simple process of refinement, and you can use it in every area of your life. Judging only makes the process uncomfortable. It does not expedite it or make things happen faster. In fact, it decidedly decreases your performance in any situation. This is all an integral part of deliberate thinking.

CHAPTER 6

HeartMath

Who's in Control, Your Heart or Your Brain?

A book on how our thoughts impact our life experience would not be complete without a brief discussion of HeartMath. The science conducted by the HeartMath Institute has given us new insights into how our hearts are much more than a simple muscle pumping blood. Our hearts affect our overall health, our decision making, and our state of personal happiness. HeartMath's research into the mind-body-heart connection is quite deep and continues to mature, and it would require much more than this short chapter to share it all. However, in my travels, I have noticed that many people have never heard of this institute despite the fact that its research has been around for over thirty years. Doc Childre founded the nonprofit HeartMath Institute in 1990. His clinical research on emotional physiology and self-regulation has been published and reviewed in scientific journals, and it has been presented at scientific conferences worldwide.

He has written twelve books to date, including *The Heart-Math Solution* and *From Chaos to Coherence*, and he created the award-winning emWave heart-rhythm coherence feedback technologies, which I use myself.

Childre's work with HeartMath has been featured on the NBC *Today Show*, ABC *World News Tonight*, CBS's *The Early Show*, CNN's *Headline News*, Discover.com, *ARS Technica*, *MacWorld*, *Information Week*, the *Daily Beast*, *Harvard Business Review*, *Business 2.0*, *Prevention* magazine, *Psychology Today*, *Golf* magazine, PGA.com, *Cosmopolitan*, *Self*, *Men's Fitness*, *Men's Health*, the *Washington Post*, *USA Today*, the *Wall Street Journal*, and many other publications and media around the world. Doc Childre also coauthors a blog with Deborah Rozman for the Living section of the *Huffington Post*.

As the institute's website states, the mission of Heart-Math is "to help people bring their physical, mental, and emotional systems into balanced alignment with their heart's intuitive guidance. This unfolds the path for becoming heart-empowered individuals who choose the way of love, which they demonstrate through compassionate care for the well-being of themselves, others, and Planet Earth."

What are some of the tenets of HeartMath? What are the discoveries of this science-backed practice and technology? HeartMath proposes there is a direct relationship and communication between our heart, our brain, and our sympathetic and parasympathetic nervous systems.

The heart has its own sort of nervous system with nerve cells that are very similar to the nerve cells found in the brain. The fetal heart begins to beat before the brain and central nervous system are finished developing. The heart sends nine times more messages to the brain than the brain sends to the heart. Because of that, many times when we think of something, that thought has come from a feeling that originated in the heart, which was then communicated to the brain and experienced as a thought. Also, the heart emanates a very large and measurable electromagnetic field that extends outside of the body up to eight feet. In other words, the frequencies of our feelings don't end at the boundaries of our body. There is data in those frequencies.

Imagine the intertwining of people's energy information in a crowded room. This connection is important to understand because what we are feeling and thinking is not as private as we may have thought. We telegraph information outside of our body, and it interacts with those around us as their energy interacts with our own. We are much more aware than we realize. What we call intuition is really our subtle awareness of what is being communicated through the interaction of our field of energy and someone else's. This is an important point to make because the interaction of someone else's energy with ours can and will trigger our thoughts. Being aware of that possibility and that process is what gives us the power to choose how we respond to that intuitive information.

The word *intuition*, like the word *difficult*, is just a label we use to describe a phenomenon. That label has unfortunately acquired a certain stigma that to some may project an image of being less than scientific fact. But our interpretation of the label does not necessarily define what it actually is. The experience of intuition is known to be real, and it can be exercised and expanded.

One sliver of awareness that we must always keep in the forefront of our minds is that reality is not defined by the limitations of our senses' ability to decode sensory information. While people have accepted this more and more, it bears repeating. Five hundred years ago, people had no way of knowing that sounds existed at frequencies outside of human hearing, since there were no technologies more powerful than the human ear. Now this is common knowledge. Human hearing is very limited in the spectrum of audible frequencies, and it is not always consistent from one person to another. I was once customizing the tonal colors produced by a Steinway grand piano for an elderly customer when she told me I needed to fix the sound of the last four notes on the top of the piano. She said, "They have no musical pitch. They just make a knocking sound." Fortunately, her husband was sitting nearby to add some levity. I delicately made her aware that they did indeed have musical pitch, but perhaps her hearing frequencies didn't extend as far as they once did. Her husband's laugh as he watched me trying to navigate the awkward moment softened my comment, and the woman laughed herself, saying, "Well, if you say it's there, it must be. I won't play any pieces that need those notes."

The same is true for wavelengths of light, such as ultraviolet and infrared, that human eyes cannot detect. No one doubts their existence today because we have technology that allows us to detect them. When I was growing up, a word like *meditation* conjured visions of Tibetan monks in saffron robes sitting for hours in a lotus position chasing an elusive religious experience. Now we know that the mechanics of meditation are very simple to learn, they are free, and anyone can do it. Meditation lowers your heart rate, normalizes your blood pressure, and slows the aging of your brain. The relationship between the heart, brain, and nervous system is no different. Lowering stress and being able to intentionally request intuitive information for better decision making improves personal health.

One of the first components of HeartMath is *entrainment*. The heart obviously produces a rhythm, and it's the most pronounced (strongest) rhythm in the body. When all the other rhythm systems in the body are in sync with the heart, it is called entrainment.

Another component is called *heart-rate variability* (HRV). HRV is the measurement of the beat-to-beat changes in the heart rate. The heart doesn't beat like a Rolex watch or musical metronome, with perfect spacing between one beat and the next. There are slight variances, and this is what we want. There is a relationship between the parasympathetic nervous system (rest and digest) and the sympathetic nervous system (fight-or-flight). As they interact with each other, that is reflected in beat-to-beat spacing. Think of HRV as being a type of feedback loop related to the heart-brain interactions and the autonomic nervous system functioning. The reason we want good HRV is because it represents the body's adaptability to changing circumstances, its flexibility. When we are in good health, we have a good heart-rate variability. We experience a sense of calmness. We perform better physically, the mind fog clears, and we sleep better. We also bounce back from stress much more quickly. On the flipside, a low HRV manifests negative aspects, such as chronic fatigue, depression, increased health risks, and much less adaptability to changing situations.

Another component of HeartMath is called *coherence*. Coherence typically describes what is logical and consistent; it is a quality that forms a unified whole. When the heart rhythm is functioning in coherency, it means that it is in control with order, harmony, and stability; both nervous system branches are synchronized. If we were to look at a graphic representation of this, we would see that the heart rate looks like a very smooth, even sine wave with no jagged edges. In this state, we experience things like increased memory and emotional stability. Most people today complain about memory issues, and a large part of that is because they are functioning in a state of incoherence.

Incoherence is the opposite of coherence; in people, it

refers to someone who is dysfunctional, whose behavior doesn't make sense. A visual graph of someone functioning in incoherence would show a very erratic, disorderly, and jagged waveform. The sympathetic and parasympathetic systems are out of sync. How does this manifest? As you would expect, we lose clarity, we feel fatigued, we have trouble processing information, and it can affect our vision, just to name a few.

So how do we know and influence which state we are creating? Your heart and your emotions are obviously intertwined. When you experience positive emotions, such as love, gratitude, or empathy, and you focus your breath on your heart, your heart-rate variability and your coherence increase. Then your heart sends that information to your brain, which impacts your nervous system.

The HeartMath Institute has a device that uses emWave technology to analyze whether someone is in a state of coherence or not. It's really useful for developing the skill of creating a coherent state on demand. The small unit clips onto the earlobe and connects to a smartphone app via Bluetooth. You then practice a simple meditation technique, and the sensor detects your level of coherency. The sensor provides a real-time moving graph of your session, and when your session is complete, you can look at an overall summary on your phone. This shows when you entered or left coherence from a time perspective and how long you were in it. The app tracks your progress and more. It's pretty amazing because the coherency response is very fast. I once put it on a friend and showed her some short clips from different YouTube videos. She was not meditating; we were just watching how the images impacted her heart's state of coherency. She was stunned to see how the images expressing happiness, compassion, and gratitude immediately pulled her heart into coherence without her feeling like she was doing anything. The disturbing images and dialogue, which are so prevalent in today's media culture, had the same effect but in a very negative way.

As I mention above, our own internal state affects others, since our electromagnetic field extends beyond our body. In one well-publicized experiment, people who were trained and skilled in creating a state of coherency within themselves were placed in a room. A fourth person who knew nothing about heart coherency was then brought in. All had measuring devices on, and in a very short period of time the fourth person's state of coherency increased significantly.

Imagine the impact if we were all aware of this and practicing it. We are so far removed from this in our ignorance of how we really work that we can't even have a neutral discussion about politics without erupting into heated debates, which produce a downward spiral of incoherence. At times we are truly prisoners of our lack of understanding, but as this information becomes more mainstream, there is real hope that people will realize that we are all connected and we are all responsible for our energetic contributions to the whole. I urge you to do your own research on HeartMath. There is plenty of information available, and it is well worth your time. If you're interested, you can find out more at HeartMath.org.

CHAPTER 7

Self-Hypnosis

*Recording Your Software
for Happiness and Success*

Most people tend to think of hypnosis as a kind of therapy for overcoming phobias, losing weight, or quitting smoking. It is certainly applicable to that. But at its core, hypnosis is the process of reprogramming responses installed in the subconscious that aren't serving our happiness. Further, we don't need someone else to hypnotize us. We can learn to hypnotize ourselves so that we can craft our own new programming. In fact, many professional hypnotists will teach their clients how to hypnotize themselves so they can reinforce what they are working on in their session.

Your subconscious mind reveals to you who *you* see yourself to be. Your subconscious mind is always aware of what you are doing, what you are saying, how you are reacting, and most importantly what you are *repeating*. It then does its best to give you back what it *believes* you want. It doesn't judge, it doesn't question, it's not creative, and it doesn't have a sense of humor. It doesn't know when you are saying something in jest versus in seriousness. You can think of it as an impartial, extremely accurate recording device. It's an exquisite feedback loop. No matter what your age, your subconscious mind still has on its hard drive the smallest details of your life all the way back into your childhood. When you ruminate on a regretful event or situation, you reinfect yourself with toxic programming, which you feed to your subconscious mind. Without thought awareness, there is no possibility of deliberate thinking. You are operating with no awareness or control over the programming you are creating or the programming you are acting out. In this state the concept of free will is an illusion. When you know what programming needs to be altered or what new programming needs to be installed, self-hypnosis is a powerful tool.

The first time I was hypnotized by a clinical hypnotherapist, I was looking for relief from a concern I had regarding experiencing motion sickness. When I was in my late teens, my uncle took me sailing. I was really enthusiastic about eventually having my own boat and doing some light cruising. It was a great opportunity to go out with him, as he was a very experienced sailor. Initially, we were sailing off the wind, meaning toward the wind but not directly into it. With the exception of a few highly evolved racing designs, such as the boats in the America's Cup, even modern sailboats cannot sail directly into the wind. Regardless, because of our relationship to the wind direction, there was a nice breeze in my face for the first several hours. It was invigorating and fun. But when we turned around to head back to the marina, we were basically sailing almost directly downwind. For a nonsailor, that means we were sailing at about the same speed that the wind was moving, so from the perspective of sitting on the boat, the air was still. That made it feel quite hot and uncomfortable. On top of that there was a lot of activity with other boats that Saturday afternoon, which made the surface of the water rough with intervals of varying swells. Those two factors combined were the perfect recipe for motion sickness, and it didn't take long to make an uninitiated person start to feel queasy. I won't go into the less-than-pleasant details, but I will say it was a long ride back to the dock. Then it was another twenty-four hours before I started feeling more like myself. The experience made quite an impression on me, one I definitely didn't want to repeat. I didn't sail again for quite some time, but despite the experience I didn't lose my interest in it.

A number of years later I decided it was time to get into sailing with my own boat. I began sailing with some fellow sailors, and I looked for a boat big enough to cruise on for at least a week at a time. As I started sailing again, I noticed I had a low-level anxiety and fear of becoming seasick. I was constantly doing an internal mental scan, asking myself how I was feeling. I knew this was not good, since constant worrying itself could even bring it on. Hypnosis seemed like a good way to free myself from ruminating on something I couldn't consciously control. If I couldn't stop on a conscious level, maybe I needed to go deeper.

Like many people who have never been hypnotized, I had some preconceived ideas about what that experience feels like. Based on what's presented in movies and TV, I assumed you had no choice but to obey, so someone could make you act like a chicken or anything else ridiculous. In fact, when under hypnosis, you don't lose your identity, your sense of right and wrong, or your ability to make your own decisions. You are always in control and can easily bring yourself out of it at any moment regardless of what the hypnotist is saying. Indeed, we all go in and out of a hypnotic state on our own multiple times during the day without realizing it.

It helped that I knew my hypnotherapist personally. She was a client of mine, and also a registered nurse, so there was a trust factor already in place. She said she could absolutely help me with what I wanted to accomplish. To start, she had me sit in a reclining chair and take a few slow, deep breaths, but things did not go in the direction that I assumed. She did not repeat something like, "You will not get seasick, you will not get seasick." In fact, she never mentioned motion sickness at all. Instead, she took me back into my childhood, and this is where things got really interesting.

Under hypnosis, I initially returned to when I was two and a half years old and in the first house that my family lived in. I knew this was my age because she asked me and I told her, and I was very certain. I was also certain about the house, even though I don't have any conscious memory of it because we moved before I was three. However, in this state, I could see everything. I stood in the living room and told her what colors the walls were, what colors the rug was, the pattern of the fabric on the sofa, the location of the stairs, and on and on. I was surprised at how detailed the experience was. Regardless of what she asked me, I could look around and answer her questions easily.

I returned to other moments in my childhood, and we eventually discovered part of the trigger for my motion sickness. When I was growing up during the 1960s and 1970s, my family spent our summer vacations camping. I have two sisters, and because we were on the road for long hours, my father had a very clever idea to convert the very back of our station wagon into a third seat. Only later was this option offered by car manufacturers. Since my sisters preferred the regular back seat, I most often sat in the far back, which I liked. Looking out the window and becoming immersed in my imagination was a wonderful way to spend the hours of driving.

This seating arrangement had one shortcoming. The brain does not like getting visual cues looking backward while one's body is moving forward. It's very confusing to our kinesthetic system because the visual information does not match what our body is feeling. For me, it wasn't such a problem just motoring down the highway, but when we were traveling over mountains and going back and forth through switchbacks, I would get motion sickness. At times, I felt so bad that my father would have to pull over so I could get out of the car until my nausea subsided. It never occurred to anyone what was actually causing the problem. I was just getting carsick. Some people are more prone to it than others.

I had completely forgotten about those childhood experiences until I was under hypnosis, and I remembered how I had become fearful of getting sick. The sailing experience had retriggered that fear without me even knowing it. Yet even while I was under hypnosis, it was clear that I was a bit conflicted. That is, I loved being in the far back seat. That was a really happy feeling, and yet that happy feeling was also associated with an unhappy one, experiencing motion sickness. Sailing was similar. It was fun and I enjoyed it, but it was also associated with motion sickness and anxiety.

The hypnotist was able to wipe that installed response out and install a new response. What is interesting is that I knew what she was saying when she said it, but I can't tell you now what that was. When the session was over, she asked me how long I thought I had been hypnotized. I was sure it wasn't more than fifteen to twenty minutes. She showed me the clock, and it had been over an hour. I was stunned at how my perception of time had changed while I was under hypnosis.

Here's the end of the story: Shortly after that, I was

driving to the boat for a sail, and I realized that due to the wind velocity and the tides that afternoon, it could make for rough sailing conditions. I had the fleeting thought, "Oh, I hope I don't get sick." But as soon as I had the thought, I instantly felt this rush of calmness and happiness that basically overcame it. The experience was so pronounced that all I could think was: "Boy, this hypnosis stuff really works." I felt immune to motion sickness. Some new program she had installed was overriding that trigger, and it had lost its power. After that I was totally relaxed when I sailed, which certainly impacted my susceptibility to motion sickness, and I was no longer bothered by it.

My next experience with hypnosis, many years later, involved healing a physical injury through self-hypnosis, which became one of the most pronounced experiences that taught me how we are not our thoughts. Yes, we create some thoughts, but most we just experience, and we are often unaware that these thoughts are in control. This is something I know after forty-five years of meditation practice, but self-healing was still more of a belief. There is a fundamental difference between a "belief" and a "knowing." A knowing is internal and comes from conscious experience. A belief is external and has not been experienced yet. Whether we realize it or not, a belief exists as a possibility until it becomes a knowing. Because of this, there is usually a sliver of doubt baked into a belief. For instance, if you have learned to ride a bike, you *know* you can ride a bike. It doesn't matter how long it has been since you have been out for a ride. But if you have never ridden a bike, no matter what anyone says to convince you that you can ride a bike, there is still a small part of you that is unsure. Even if you believe it, you haven't done it yet, so you don't know.

I learned how to hypnotize myself from Marisa Peer. She is highly credentialed, and if you're interested in learning how to do this yourself, I suggest checking out her website (MarisaPeer.com), which has plenty of information and resources on the subject.

The reason I was interested in being able to hypnotize myself was because of a shoulder injury that I had sustained in 2019. It started as a mild discomfort and escalated considerably over a short period of time. The pain got to a point that over-the-counter painkillers were ineffective, and it was really impacting my sleep. It was so bad that if I rolled onto my right side while asleep, the pain would wake me up with a jolt. Around that same time, a close friend of mine was struggling with the very same symptoms. We had different personalities, and she immediately sought medical intervention. She started off with steroid shots and then physical therapy. When neither of those were effective, she finally decided to have surgery. This worked but it required quite a few weeks for recovery.

Being rather stubborn and determined to prove the power of my mind to myself, I decided to take a different path. I believed that being able to heal myself from something so uncomfortable was possible, but I didn't know it yet from my own experience. To be successful, I knew I had to get past that feeling of doubt that was very subtle but definitely there. I thought that if I could learn to hypnotize myself, I could mentally and emotionally push past the intellectual reasoning that was feeding that sliver of doubt and the feeling that I needed medical intervention of some sort. I also felt I had nothing to lose. If it worked, it would be amazing. If it didn't, I would soldier on with the understanding that, as with the early aviators, self-healing wasn't something I couldn't do or wasn't meant to do, but I just didn't have all the information yet. I made sure not to share my goal with anyone else, lest their ego get involved in the conversation and they infiltrate my confidence with their nonbelief.

The final part of the instructions for inducing the state of hypnosis was to tell your subconscious to raise one of your hands off the arm of the chair. I was sitting in a soft chair with my back erect and my forearms resting on the armrests with my palms down. I didn't want to sit there and *tell* my hand to raise up. That felt like it wouldn't work. Instead, in my mind, I saw my hand raising and tried to create the *feeling* of my hand raising.

At first it didn't feel like anything was happening, but then very slowly my hand began to raise completely on its own. I can't express in words how incredible this feeling was. "I" was definitely *not* raising my hand, and yet something, some other part of me, was. It was a very slow motion, which I noticed because I didn't feel I could intentionally raise my hand so slowly and with such precision. There was no stuttering to the motion. I was so separate from the process that it felt like I was just watching it. I felt like this was one of the most amazing things I'd ever experienced. Once my hand was raised, I then initiated the feeling of it stopping and visualized a parachute coming out and letting it float slowly back to the armrest. Again, my fingertips touched the chair so softly and with such deliberate, slow movement that I felt I couldn't have achieved it if I had tried to do it consciously. Something else was in control.

At that point I felt convinced that I was "in the vault." I had achieved access to my subconscious mind. In that place, I told it that it had created a healthy shoulder all of my life and that I didn't need to know what was causing the pain on an intellectual basis. I told my body: "The intelligence that has always been there knows what to do, so do it. Bring the shoulder back to perfect health." I then went through the process of bringing myself out of hypnosis.

I repeated this process daily, and it only took ten minutes. Within three days, there was a noticeable improvement. I began to be able to sleep through the night. Within several weeks, the pain was gone completely, and it never came back. This made perfect sense to me. When we cut our finger, we expect our body to repair it, and so we don't doubt it. When we get a cold, we expect to get over it. We expect the intelligence present in our body to take care of us without us having to get involved. It seemed reasonable to me that my body had the intelligence to correct whatever was wrong (most likely severe inflammation) if I instructed it to do so. Hypnotic programming *is* deliberate thinking. It is us intentionally creating thoughts and installing those thoughts at our deepest level. We are telling ourselves who we really are and what we are capable of. Now I no longer believe self-healing is possible; I know it's possible.

Years ago I was reading about the Chinese medical treatment of acupuncture in the hope that it might relieve some of the symptoms my mother was dealing with related to her cancer. I was surprised to find that acupuncture was originally developed in part because the Chinese did not believe in "violating" the human body, meaning surgery. Today, China has what we would call nonsurgical hospitals, and I remember seeing a video of a treatment at one of these hospitals. The patient was a woman with a malignant tumor in her stomach. She was lying on a reclined table, and two television screens behind her showed a sonogram of the tumor. One monitor showed a snapshot of the tumor before they started. The other monitor showed a real-time image of the tumor. Three practitioners stood next to the woman, and in what appeared to be a meditative state, they were chanting a phrase over and over again. The narrator said this loosely translated as "already done, already done, now, now."

While this was going on, the tumor began to shrink. It got smaller and smaller until it dissipated completely.

We in the West have been completely and constantly conditioned to feel that this is improbable, if not impossible, and we would tend to look at this with suspicion. But as I say in the introduction, monks in the East talked for centuries about having experiences during meditation that might seem impossible, and there was no way to share the authenticity of it with others. Now, brain scans and sophisticated laboratory instruments can verify that the altered states and experiences the monks described are real. The healing of this woman was possible because all of those involved *expected* it to work, just like we expect a cut on a finger to heal or a cold to go away. There was no doubt involved in their paradigm. They perhaps even viewed it as a normal procedure, just like we might have invasive surgery to remove a similar tumor. The great philosopher Plato warned of limiting our concept of reality to what the five senses are capable of. When we cast something like this off as being impossible, we become prisoners of our limited thinking.

Self-hypnosis is how we can communicate with our subconscious mind. It is one method for gaining control of writing the programs that serve our happiness and facilitate the achievement of our goals.

The subconscious mind is the student. The conscious mind instructs, and the subconscious mind records, stores, and performs the programs that we give it. It is the hard drive of behaviors. It is always working, and just because we aren't paying attention to what we are instructing doesn't mean it isn't *learning*. It learns through repetition, and it is much more powerful than the conscious mind in terms of performance. The subconscious mind can process upwards of forty million bits of data per second, while the conscious mind can process only around four million bits per second. This is why, when we enter fight-or-flight, we automatically and involuntarily switch over to the subconscious mind because it can perform survival tasks automatically. It acts much faster than if we had to consciously *think* about what to do. It is not creative, though. Only the conscious mind has that power.

An interesting example of this is the game of golf. Golfers are taught to have a single "swing thought" during their swing process, since this occupies the left brain and allows the subconscious mind to make the swing. If this doesn't happen, the golfer can become almost paralyzed mentally as the conscious mind tries to keep up with all the dots that need to be connected to execute the swing. The subconscious mind does it effortlessly because of its performance advantage.

Initially, the conscious mind learns the complex physical movements of the golf swing, taking in the information through formal instruction. Then, through repetition, the conscious mind basically *shows* the subconscious mind what to do during a particular swing. At that point, the golfer could just voluntarily step back and let the subconscious run the calculations to produce the swing for any given shot. But the conscious mind doesn't want to let go of being in control. This is the more esoteric side of the game. It's evokes the line in *Star Wars* where Obi Wan's spirit tells Luke to "let go and trust your feelings." The swing thought basically ties the golfer's conscious mind up with something to focus on so it gets out of the way of the subconscious mind and lets it control the body. Believe me, it is easier said than done.

The language of the subconscious mind is *images* and *emotions*. That is why just talking to it in a normal waking state doesn't really work. It doesn't notice what we are saying because it needs the information in a different format. It doesn't judge content. It observes what is happening to you and what your *interpretation* of that is (images and emotions). It pays attention to what reactions and responses you repeat and then installs that information as programming, which is ready for recall in a microsecond without conscious intervention. Why? Because habits are very efficient. They require almost no processing power. They can be executed instantly because the data and the *decisions* are already made. If you think of your brain as a computer processor, it has a limited amount of RAM; there is only so much processing it can handle at one time. When you learn something new, it requires a lot more processing than when you repeat something you have mastered. When my two-year-old grandson was learning to use a spoon to feed himself, it took all of his concentration. His brain was running full out to coordinate everything that had to happen to get that spoonful of food up to his mouth without spilling. But this action is now automatic.

Our subconscious mind is designed to make repeated actions and reactions into habits. In other words, our *behaviors* are habitualized, like a golf swing after hundreds of repetitions. The same process applies to physical and mental actions. This is why neuroscientists say that we only operate from our conscious mind about 5 percent of the time. The rest of the time, the subconscious is just running programs fired off by stimulus.

You can live your intentions, or you can live your programs. The process of being mentally and emotionally present in the moment, of being where your feet are, so to speak, is fundamental in deliberate thinking. The more skilled you are at that, the more you operate from your conscious mind, which is what we all want. How much more, we don't know, but it can surely grow higher than 5 percent. We need our subconscious mind to survive, and it is an incredibly powerful tool when we are consciously and intentionally creating the programs installed there using deliberate thinking. By developing your skill level of thought awareness, you can monitor what programing is installed by noticing how any situation makes you feel. You can empower yourself by adjusting your interpretation so that what your subconscious mind observes is what you want. You can accelerate and facilitate that process through learning self-hypnosis.

CHAPTER 8

If You Could Do Anything You Wanted

Creating the Best Thoughts in Difficult Situations

I once worked with a woman who was in a very difficult relationship. Things had gotten to a point where she and her partner had sought professional counseling. In one of our conversations, she revealed to me that she dreaded the sessions. When I asked her to elaborate, she said that her partner would intimidate her to a point of anxiety where she struggled to participate in the session. She said his intimidation was intentional and that he viewed it as a sign of superior intelligence and almost a craft he possessed for controlling her. I asked her: "If I could touch you on the head with a magic wand and make you become any person you wanted in your next session, who would that be?" She thought for a moment and answered, "I really have no idea." I responded, "That's the question you need to answer. If you're not clear about that when you're in a calm state of mind and away from the situation, you're not going to be able to figure it out when you're in it."

This is such a simple concept, and yet over and over again I find that when people feel out of control in a particular situation or circumstance, they exhaust all of their energy immersed in the emotional content of the thoughts that the situation brings on. Their *interpretation* of the circumstance is a playback of what they have unknowingly told themselves over and over again. There is nothing *deliberate* about their response. As I say, there is a difference between reacting and responding. I know that we use these two words interchangeably, but from my perspective, a reaction has no conscious intention behind it. A response is deliberate and thought out.

To build a skill, the foundation of the process starts with gaining the perspective of the observer, the one who is really us, the one who notices the thought process but can remain outside of it. We should use our mind and not allow our mind to use us. Everything is possible when we are in that place. That is when we truly have free will. That is when we have the privilege of choice. This is admittedly easier said than done, but much of that stems from the fact that we were never taught to operate this way. Most of us are at the beginning of the learning curve.

Just because we have the opportunity and the ability to choose doesn't mean that the process is easy. When someone makes that comment to me, I usually respond, "What does that have to do with it?" Lots of things are not easy. Learning to play an instrument is not easy, but it enriches us our whole life. Becoming fully present, detached, and in control in a really uncomfortable situation could be described as difficult, and it takes practice, but it feels so much better than experiencing fear and negative emotions that we have no control over. In fact, most of the things worth achieving in life are accompanied by a sense of difficulty. It's just a normal part of the process and should be seen as such and not as a deterrent.

I also remind people that words like *easy* and *difficult* are labels we attach to describe how an experience feels. If it's easy, it feels good; if it's not easy, if feels not so good. But how it feels is mostly dependent on how we interpret it and thus define it. What one person feels is difficult or fearful, another person may interpret very differently. For the most part, situations and circumstances just are. We create what they *seem* to be.

That may sound like an oversimplification, but is the fear someone feels in a job interview absolute, or is it just frightening because the person lacks the skills to give them confidence in the situation? Is confronting a certain person inherently fearful, or is it just fearful to the individual? I have known situations where one person is very intimidated by someone, and yet another person has no trouble putting that same person in their place if need be and actually enjoys it. As far as life-threatening situations, I agree that we can't pass them off as being neutral. However, we are always more effective and comfortable if we control our thoughts rather than letting them control us. That depends on how we interpret situations, so do we possess the skill to control that?

The movie analogy I would use is *The Terminator*. Arnold Schwarzenegger's character observes situations, *analyzes* the data on his internal screen, and independent of any emotion, crafts an appropriate response. Of course, that is fiction. He's a robot and we're not. But removing a preprogrammed and habitual emotional response from a situation is a process, and with preparation and practice, you can become quite good at it.

The woman in the counseling sessions provides a good example of how to build the skill of interpreting situations the way we want so that our experience of them is more in line with what works best for us. I told the woman that her situation offered her an ideal opportunity to work on the skill of interpretation because the sessions were recurring and predictable. She knew *when* they were going to happen, and that gave her a bit of an edge in terms of getting out in front of her learned response.

If you walk into a dark room and someone you can't see and don't expect suddenly grabs your arm, it will surely startle and unsettle you. But if you were told that, after taking four steps into the room, someone would grab you to try to frighten you, that same situation would lose almost all of its power. You would know when, where, and what would happen. I told the woman that she already knew what her partner's behavior would be during the next counseling session, but he only *thought* he knew what hers would be. That's because he was just as much a prisoner of a learned response as she was. Over and over again, he had intimidated her in their relationship, and his subconscious had observed and installed that dynamic onto *his* hard drive. Because of that, he would expect her to react in a predictable way to his behavior.

I asked her again what her ideal response would be in this situation, and she was still unsure. So I suggested she focus on the thought, "I am not going to allow him to touch my inner peace." I told her that would be her focus, and then I continued:

> It's very simple. That is where *your* attention is going to be. Instead of paying attention to the hurtful and manipulating things he is saying, I want you to *notice* when he starts in with his predictable behavior right on cue. That will be your trigger to focus on being the observer of yourself and to watch what thoughts and feelings *your* subconscious mind brings up in response to his behavior. *You* are *not* those thoughts and those reactions. You are just watching them as they show up. You look at them with as much detachment as you can muster. You view them as if you are just watching and learning what your present programing for such a situation is. That's all.

When we next spoke, she told me that she was amazed at how such a simple shift in attention had diffused his power over her. She had *believed* the strategy would work, but after experiencing it, this had shifted to *knowing*. That perspective gave her the inspiration and enthusiasm to keep working at it.

When you are just beginning the practice of this skill, it is important to make a very conscious promise to yourself that you will not judge your performance. That is pointless and unfair at this stage. I can't say that it is not productive because it is. Every action *produces* something, but it doesn't always produce comfort and self-confidence. Judgment is an easy trap to fall into when you begin the process of developing any new skill.

I told the woman that the next step was to craft her own response to her partner's behavior so that she didn't have to figure it out in the moment. That would help her avoid involuntarily reacting unconsciously to his behavior. This is really no different than when a parent restricts their young child from having something that they want, and the child predictably throws a tantrum. The parent *expects* the behavior, and because of that, they are immune to it. They are not in a reactive state, but instead they are more in control and can choose to execute a planned response. In the safety of our counseling session, the woman would *choose* to be immune to his words. She would consciously make that decision outside of the emotionally charged environment of the session.

I wanted her to understand that her anxiety-filled reaction was just a program that she had unknowingly practiced (or repeated) to the point that it had become a very dependable skill. Because she had mastered it, she executed it with effortless ease whenever her subconscious received the stimulus. Let me say it again: That subconscious behavior is *not* who *you* are! Your goal, like this woman's, is to craft a response that, with repetition, will become just as automatic, but it will be more representative of who you want to be in any particular situation.

Your subconscious mind does not differentiate between internal and external stimulus. It is just watching and noticing how you feel in relation to the situation and then recording it for future reference. It doesn't "think." It doesn't say, "I know you don't want to react this way because it makes you feel awful, so I'll tweak it a bit." The subconscious just observes the stimulus and runs the program for this event. I know it doesn't always feel this way, but you never really lose control. You just don't know that you have control. As I say, we tend to notice the situations we are not very good at handling much more than the ones we are. That's understandable because we don't experience a sense of *resistance* when we are engaged in an activity where we have achieved a high level of skill. Those situations just flow, and we experience them as being more or less effortless.

Here is a simple process to follow: First, identify specifically what you want to work on. Choose one specific situation that you feel you need to interpret differently to improve your comfort level and to feel more in control. With regard to all personal transformation, it's always a best practice to limit your focus, so choose a situation that embodies what I call the four S words: simple, small, short, and slow (which I discuss in *The Practicing Mind*). Pick one situation and simplify your effort by breaking down your response into smaller sections. Don't say, "I'm going to completely change my responses in all situations that relate to a particular challenge." Pledge something more like: "I will change one aspect of my response in one specific situation and only for the first ten minutes."

Set realistic goals because success breeds confidence, inspiration, and emotional stamina. Intentionally underestimate yourself rather than biting off too much; avoid delusions of grandeur. Work at the new interpretation for short periods, and understand that repetition is king in skill development. Further, ensure you have some downtime in between repetitions. In that way, it's no different than physical exercise. During your execution, if you feel you are still in control, then you can give yourself permission to push a little farther, while understanding that you can change your mind. If you do, it is not a sign of weakness; it's just a sign that you are in touch with yourself and recognizing where your threshold is at this moment.

I find that when I'm trying to work at change like this, there is a point where I peak in my performance. Your feelings will tell you when you reach this point, and when you do, let yourself relax your effort. You are pushing against a response that is deeply habitualized and has a lot of strength. That's only a negative when you are trying to change it. When that same mechanism is working for you, it can be a powerful ally.

This is basic peak-performance work. In sports psychology, there is a mantra: "You can't learn and perform at the same time." When you first start this process, you are learning what works best for creating change, so you are basically in a stage of gathering data. Look at it like that. When you are gathering information, don't judge performance. That wouldn't make any sense. As I mention earlier, you do, observe, and correct (DOC); that's all. There is only execution and analysis of observed results to form the next execution, like a basketball player shooting foul shots. If you push too long, you will get fatigued mentally and emotionally, and then your execution will suffer. This will needlessly erode your confidence in your abilities.

This is true for both mental and physical skill development. I have watched people hit so many balls at the golf range that they physically exhaust themselves. When that happens, their mechanics begin to break down, and they start to unknowingly ingrain bad habits into their swing. They erroneously think that by pushing themselves longer they will overcome this and keep moving forward, but in reality they can be sabotaging their progress. The fatigue creates errant shots, which make them doubt their progress and feel they must work even harder and longer. It's a downward spiral, and they leave the practice session feeling terrible. That can be easily avoided by setting reasonable goals you know you can achieve. The more advanced you become in any skill, the more expanded your concept of what is possible becomes, so relax and enjoy the process of mastery.

The mental skill of *deliberate interpretation* is no different. It will serve you the rest of your life and in all areas of your life, so relax and repeat the process without judgment. Let the mastery flow toward you at its own pace. It's a good opportunity to work on the skill of self-patience. When you *notice* yourself feeling impatient, that's your trigger to realize that you are experiencing a learned interpretation that says, "This is the program to run when something is taking longer than I thought it would."

Working at personal transformation is endless, so accept that as a blessing. Your ability to expand is infinite, so you will never "get there." This can be a very difficult and perhaps uncomfortable concept for us with a Western background. We all have way too much to do, and that creates a hunger for "closure." We want to see tasks completed, accomplished, and off of our plate so we can stop thinking about them and move on to the next task. We want the food shopping done, the report at work done, the stressful meeting over with. We're not comfortable looking at something as never really done, and yet we all have things in our life that we accept in this way. We accept that we have to brush our teeth every day and that we have to exercise our whole life. We know that if we skip brushing or exercising once, or for a few years, we don't then say, "That's it, I'm finished. I no longer need to brush or exercise for the rest of my life." These are ongoing, necessary activities for living a healthy life. Developing the power and skill to deliberately direct your thinking and thus your interpretations of various situations puts you much more in control. It is an ongoing, necessary activity that is worth the effort. *You* are worth the effort.

After you have decided on a specific area to work on, ask yourself: "If I could do anything I want in this situation, what would that be?" Next, *write it down*. This is another basic rule of personal peak performance. When we ponder things in our heads, they exist in an abstract form and also in a state of indecision. Every thought we have creates another thought, and in microseconds, overthinking begins to cascade in multiple directions, causing us to lose focus. At the same time, as our mind runs amuck visiting different scenarios, we experience the emotional content of those scenarios, which impacts our clarity.

Articulating your objective and your process for achieving that objective on paper forces you to be clear, to distill the various components necessary to be successful. This is when you make decisions about exactly what your objective is for the specific situation and what is necessary to achieve it. It gives you a solid target to aim at, and that is a very powerful asset. You eliminate most if not all of the decisions you would have to make on the fly when under stress. Your cognitive acuity is much higher when you are removed from the situation. Having a target that you have chosen in a state of calmness gives you confidence, and it becomes something to latch onto in the heat of the moment when the habitual response you are pushing against shows up.

This is why professional golfers have what they call a "preshot routine." This could be viewed as a sort of "safe space" to retreat to, a familiar place where, even though they are under stress, they know exactly what to do. It helps to disempower learned behaviors that may diminish the player's ability to execute a skill level that through practice they have earned. Their mind is quieter and more focused because no decisions need to be made here. They've already made them when they were clear and calm. When you operate this way, the decisions driving your actions come from conscious and deliberate thinking, and they are more in line with your will.

What if something you didn't count on blindsides you? Well, that's no different. Ask yourself in the moment: "If I could do whatever I want, be whoever I want, respond however I want, what would that be?" Accept that you can only work with the data you have at the time. If a situation you have never encountered or didn't expect comes up, you can only control so much. Some speculation on your part is unavoidable, so adjust your expectations accordingly and without judgment. After all, in an unexpected situation, you are more in learning mode than in performing mode.

One thing you *can* control is how you appear outwardly while you process the information internally. That can be very challenging, but if you have no idea of what your preferred response *looks* like, it's probably not going to end well. Like the woman going into the counseling situation unprepared, you are being controlled by circumstances instead of the other way around.

Remember, when it comes to practicing, for the most part the brain does not differentiate between something really happening and a simulation. In the 1970s, Olympic athletes participated in experiments where they closed their eyes and practiced their routines in their minds. What researchers found was that the brain fired off all the same signals and stored the reps as if the routines were actually happening. This is why pilots spend so much time in simulations to prepare for emergencies, both predictable and unforeseen. I can tell you that it definitely works. When you get clear on your preferred interpretation for a specific scenario, spend some time rehearsing it in your mind. You will be amazed at how that practice shows up when you need it most.

CHAPTER 9

Cheating Discipline Is the Pursuit of Emptiness

Joy Comes from the Process of Achieving

W e spend about 98 percent of our life in the *process* of achieving our goals. We only spend a very short moment realizing them. My daughter recently finished running her first marathon in New York, and I was there close to the finish line. She had trained for three months, and when the day of the marathon came, she had still not run as far as the race required her to. Her training was disciplined and organized. She had a target time for her mile speed, and during her training she continued with her full-body workouts. She practiced running in the rain, when it was hot, when it was cold, and when she really didn't feel like it.

We don't pay enough attention to the fact that the rush we experience when we step across the finish line is created by the process of getting there. We need our goals. They define our targets, but it's our interpretation of the process that creates our experience of achieving our goals.

If I had taken a piece of chalk, drawn a line on the street, and told my daughter, "There's the finish line. Go ahead and step over it," the experience would have meant nothing. Most of us know this, and yet we discard that knowledge in our daily practice. We still want the goal now.

I see this mindset virtually everywhere. In golf, I routinely see people with horrific swing mechanics who will spend hundreds of dollars on just one club that is supposed to overcome their lack of fundamentals and proper practice and let them hit the ball as if they were well schooled and had practiced many hours. I was once paired with someone who had thousands of dollars tied up in his clubs. They represented the latest technology available, and according to the marketing, they were supposed to cure many swing deficiencies. On the first tee he hit his ball so far off line, it went into the parking lot and broke the windshield on someone's car. He turned to me and said, "I tried to buy a good swing, but apparently it didn't work."

There is songwriting software that figures out the chords you should use to compose your song; no need to explore ideas, it's already done for you. Are you even a part of the process at that point when the computer writes the music? In *The Practicing Mind*, I wrote about how during my days in the piano service business the "fun machines," as they were called, were popular. A keyboard played most of the music, and you just followed along pushing one key at a time based on these gigantic notes on the page. It was supposed to give someone who couldn't play, and didn't want to exert the discipline necessary to learn, the experience of playing ... well, sort of. After arriving home, those keyboards were rarely used because the experience was empty.

The process of achieving your goals is a feedback loop because, during the process, you are building a relationship with the spirit of the goal itself. For example, during my twenty-five-year tenure as the senior concert piano technician at a major performing arts theater known as the Grand Opera House, I met and spoke with many of the world's best musicians. Their perspective about practice was that it was a process of building a relationship with their instrument, with the composer whose work they were performing (if they were in the classical genre), and with the spirit of music itself. They commented that you had to be comfortable being alone with your thoughts and with the process of achieving your goals and that the time spent was absolutely essential. It was manifested in the delivery of your performance. That is true whether you are playing music, running a race, or achieving more personal power in a difficult situation.

Practice and discipline are tied together. My jazz piano teacher told me two things I never forgot. One was, "The reason we practice is so that our worst performance is acceptable." And the other was, "In order to be free in the art, you must first be a slave to the process." Practice breaks down the technical barriers that are present in any execution, and it brings freedom of expression. Again, this is not just about music. When you enter a difficult meeting or are confronted with a fearful situation, your practice will bring you the freedom to execute your will effortlessly. This sensation is pure joy. You feel powerful because you are. Your life is more representative of who you want to be. You are not governed by your lack of skill in any particular situation. When you try to jump past the process, you deprive yourself of all that it creates in you.

If you become attached to the moment when you reach a goal, you immediately become at war with the process of achieving it. That is why you experience a feeling of resistance to being where you are now, where your feet are, as they say, and long for the moment of achievement. But the experience of that moment is in direct proportion to what it took to get there. When you surrender to this truth, and you realize that the process forms what you will experience in the moment of achievement, you lose the sense of impatience to "get there." This is deliberate thinking. It's choosing what programs you will install on your hard drive, and this determines what you will experience as you accomplish your goals.

CHAPTER 10

It's Just a Thought, but It Should Be Your Thought

Who Is Getting into Your Head?

In the 1950s, a technology used in drive-in movies showed short bursts of images on the screen. These images were of popcorn, hot dogs, and other items sold at the concession counter. The bursts were so short that the conscious mind did not pick them up, but the subconscious mind did, and this caused people to crave the snacks, which of course turned into action as people went to make a purchase.

The government made this illegal because it manipulated people's behavior without their knowledge or consent. Today we don't seem to function under the same set of rules. For example, an experimental technology called "targeted dream incubation" might one day be used, according to one of the corporate participants, to compel the subconscious to dream about a product.

Essentially, in the research, subjects are shown a short video with images and an audio track, in which a subconscious stimulus is associated with the images, such as a sound. Then, the stimulus is played while the person is asleep, hopefully causing them to dream about the product. How would that work in practice? I can only speculate, but the technology could be incorporated into a commercial. Because many people sleep with their smartphone by their bed, a sound could be pinged to their phone during sleeping hours, and this might stimulate the response. It sounds crazy, but is it any crazier than what was being done in the 1950s? It's just using updated technology.

Tristan Harris, a former Google employee, has been very outspoken about how we are about ten years into a technology plan to capture our attention. His testimonies before Congress give some examples, which are disturbing, to say the least. Current corporate research is exploring how to use human psychology and dopamine hits from the brain to create addictive behaviors, and no one outside the benefactors seems to be paying attention. We already know that our devices are listening to us. I was talking on the phone to a friend recently. She had her phone on speaker and said she was craving crab cakes, but she couldn't get them locally. I mentioned a national vendor that sold and shipped them in large quantities frozen. During the discussion, her roommate was sitting in the room working on a computer, and before we hung up, the roommate had received a coupon from the vendor. Sometimes, after looking up an item on Google, the next time I go to YouTube, videos about the product are in my feed.

There is a war going on for our attention and for access to our thoughts and emotions. That was always the plan for the concept of social media: Addict people to their screens and then you have their eyes and minds. This has been very successful. Two different people looking at the same Facebook page will see the posts in a different order because the algorithms know which posts will push their buttons. The goal is to motivate people so that they can't resist looking at their screen when they hear their text alert. While watching a marathon my daughter was in, I observed other runners texting while they were running. We're in trouble. After months of marathon training, could these runners not put their screens away for two hours so they could be fully present to the race itself?

We must all realize the power our minds have with the thoughts we are creating. They create our perception of who we are and how we are connected to everyone else. To get to the place where we can reach our true potential and contribute to a better world for all, we must first get to the place where we experience the understanding: "I am not my thoughts. Some I create, but many happen to me without my permission or intention." It is from here that we are released from the prison that our mind can create. It is here that we can truly experience ourselves as the magnificent beings we were always meant to be.

Notes

Page 8, *For example, I recently read a study on the different brain wave states*: David Dobbs, "Zen Gamma," *Scientific American*, April 1, 2005, https://www.scientificamerican.com/article /zen-gamma.

Page 10, *In 1985, an eight-week series appeared on public television*: *The Day the Universe Changed*, directed by Richard Reisz, written by James Burke (1985, BBC Four), https://www.bbc .co.uk/programmes/b04l6w0d.

Page 59, *"You are a very fast flier, aren't you?"*: Richard Bach, *Jonathan Livingston Seagull* (1970; repr., New York: Scribner, 2014), 45.

Page 73, *The science conducted by the HeartMath Institute has given us*: All studies and information are from the HeartMath Institute, https://www.heartmath.org.

About the Author

Thomas M. Sterner is the founder and CEO of the Practicing Mind Institute (TomSterner.com). As a successful entrepreneur, he is considered an expert in present-moment functioning (PMF). He is a popular and in-demand speaker and coach who works with industry groups and high-performance individuals of all ages, including athletes, coaches, and CEOs, freeing them to operate effectively in high-stress situations so that they can break through to new levels of mastery.

As an expert present-moment functioning coach, Thomas has brought clarity to thousands worldwide regarding how they can achieve their goals with less effort, in the least amount of time, while enjoying the process. Top media outlets such as NPR, Fox News, and *Forbes* have sought his advice. He is the author of the international bestseller *The Practicing Mind: Developing Focus and Discipline in Your Life* (New World Library, 2012) and *Fully Engaged: Using the Practicing Mind in Daily Life* (New World Library, 2016). His books have been translated into nine languages, and he is one of New World Library's top-ten bestselling authors.

Prior to founding the Practicing Mind Institute, he served as the chief concert piano technician for a major performing arts center preparing instruments for the most demanding performances. During his twenty-five-year tenure as a high-level technician, he personally worked for industry giants such as Van Cliburn, Pavarotti, André Watts, Ray Charles, Fleetwood Mac, Bonnie Raitt, Tony Bennett, Wynton Marsalis, and many more. This provided him with a unique opportunity to converse with some of the most disciplined minds on how they approach the process of "practicing," the art of skill-building, and dealing with stress when they need to perform at their highest level. He lives in Delaware.